FIVE DAYS
IN NOVEMBER

FIVE DAYS
IN NOVEMBER

CLINT HILL
AND LISA McCUBBIN

GALLERY BOOKS

NEW YORK · LONDON · TORONTO · SYDNEY · NEW DELHI

G

Gallery Books
A Division of Simon & Schuster, Inc.
1230 Avenue of the Americas
New York, NY 10020

First Gallery Books paperback edition September 2014

GALLERY BOOKS and colophon are registered trademarks of Simon & Schuster, Inc.

For information about special discounts for bulk purchases, please contact
Simon & Schuster Special Sales at 1-866-506-1949 or business@simonandschuster.com.

The Simon & Schuster Speakers Bureau can bring authors to your live event.
For more information or to book an event, contact the Simon & Schuster Speakers Bureau
at 1-866-248-3049 or visit our website at www.simonspeakers.com.

Text designed by Paul Dippolito

Manufactured in the United States of America

10   9   8   7   6

Library of Congress Cataloging-in-Publication Data is available.
    Hill, Clint.
       Five days in November / Clint Hill and Lisa McCubbin.
          pages cm
       Summary: "*The New York Times* bestselling authors of *Mrs. Kennedy and Me* share the stories behind the five infamous, tragic days surrounding JFK's assassination—alongside revealing and iconic photographs—published in remembrance of the beloved president on the fiftieth anniversary of his death. Clint Hill will forever be remembered as the lone secret service agent who jumped onto the car after President Kennedy was shot, clinging to its sides as it sped toward the hospital. Even now, decades after JFK's presidency, the public continues to be fascinated with the Kennedys—America's royal family. To mark the fiftieth anniversary of President John F. Kennedy's assassination, Hill recounts his indelible memories of those five days leading up to, and after, that tragic day in November 1963. Hill, as Jackie's guard, experienced those days firsthand. Alongside the famous photos everyone is familiar with, Hill provides a moment-to-moment narration evoking the feelings and emotions behind the images—clearing up the persistent conspiracy misconceptions along the way. He also shows us the little-seen photos of Jackie both before and after the terrible event, describing the poignant moments they shared, during that pivotal moment in history. Told movingly by a man who still wishes he could undo it all, *Five Days in November* is a rare and deeply personal look at the assassination that affected the entire world and changed the United States forever"—Provided by publisher.
       1. Kennedy, John F. (John Fitzgerald), 1917–1963—Assassination. 2. Kennedy, John F. (John Fitzgerald), 1917–1963—Death and burial. 3. Onassis, Jacqueline Kennedy, 1929–1994. 4. United States. Secret Service—Officials and employees—Biography. I. McCubbin, Lisa. II. Title.
    E842.9.H55 2013
       973.922092—dc23   2013019272
    ISBN 978-1-4767-3149-0
    ISBN 978-1-4767-3150-6 (pbk)
    ISBN 978-1-4767-3151-3 (ebook)

In memory of

President
John Fitzgerald Kennedy

May 29, 1917–November 22, 1963

Contents

Introduction

It makes no difference how old you are, or what you have experienced, there are times in your life that affect you so deeply that, no matter what you do, no matter how hard you try to erase them, your mind will never let the memories fade. For me, there were five days in November 1963, when I was thirty-one years old, that are seared into my mind and soul. In the blink of an eye, everything changed, and in the fifty years since, those days remain the defining period of my life. As fate would have it, the photos snapped by journalists, witnesses, and bystanders during those five days are like the scrapbook that is in my mind. I was thrust onto the pages of history and have spent the majority of my life keeping silent about what I witnessed.

Recently, however, I have come to realize that the grief I've held inside for half a century is shared by nearly everyone who was alive at that time, and that those days marked a defining period not just for me but for all of us. It has been a reluctant journey, but now, despite how painful it is, still, to relive those days, I understand that my memories are important to history.

President Kennedy's election in 1960 coincided with the blossoming of a new era in American history. There was a marked difference between the outgoing leader—seventy-year-old President Dwight D. Eisenhower, a five-star general, a grandfatherly figure—and the incoming forty-three-year-old President John F. Kennedy, with his quick wit and charismatic smile. In his eloquent and stirring inaugural address, President Kennedy stated, "Let the word go forth from this time and place, to friend and foe alike, that the torch has been passed to a new generation of Americans . . ."

His words rang true to those of us in that younger generation. We could see his vision. Financially, we were doing better than our parents had done, the economy was growing, and even for those who were struggling, there was hope and promise ahead.

This was also the beginning of the television age—a time when *Father Knows Best* and *Leave It to Beaver* idealized the wholesome traditional families of the 1950s, while the nightly news brought images of civil rights clashes into people's living rooms. The presidential debates between Kennedy and Nixon were the first ever shown on television, and the stark contrast between the younger, handsome Kennedy's charming ease and Nixon's apparent discomfort arguably tipped the election in Kennedy's favor in the last critical weeks of the election.

President Kennedy recognized the power of television and its ability to connect him with the American people. He was the first president to conduct live televised press conferences without delay or editing, and people loved them. His quick-witted bantering with the press was so entertaining that college students and shift workers would rush home to tune in, while housewives scheduled their ironing in front of the television.

The American public was also enamored with the president's beautiful young wife, Jacqueline, and their two children, Caroline and John. Clothing manufacturers produced copies of the first lady's classic suits and pillbox hats so the average American woman could dress in "Jackie style," while the press clamored for photos and tidbits of information about the family's private activities. With their family's private plane, and homes in Hyannis Port and Palm Beach, the Kennedys' lifestyle was one that most Americans could only dream about. People couldn't get enough of them. They were more popular than any television or movie stars; Jack and Jackie Kennedy were American royalty.

As the young American president and his elegant wife traveled outside the country, their popularity spread around the world. It was awe inspiring to see hundreds of thousands, and sometimes millions, of people in foreign countries standing along a motorcade route just to get a glimpse of this man whose vision for freedom, liberty, and peace resonated with people of all walks of life, of all different races and religions. As the first Catholic American president, Kennedy was held in especially high esteem by fellow Catholics, and his photograph hung prominently in living rooms, shops, and restaurants around the world.

During the Kennedy administration, I was an up-close-and-personal witness to what later would be called "Camelot." On November 21, 1963, I accompanied President and Mrs. Kennedy to Texas as part of their Secret Service detail. As Special Agent in Charge of the First Lady's Detail, it was my responsibility to protect Jacqueline Kennedy, and I was with her constantly.

On November 22, when shots were fired during the motorcade in Dallas, there was a Secret Service agent who jumped on the back of the car, attempting to protect President and Mrs. Kennedy.

That was me.

Unbeknownst to me, an Associated Press photographer named James Altgens was on Elm Street in Dealey Plaza at the time of the assassination. He heard the shots, saw me run, and snapped a photo just as I climbed onto the back of the presidential limousine. That evening, and the next day, this photograph ran on the front pages of newspapers all over the world. From that point on, I would forever be known as the Secret Service agent who jumped on the back of the car. And while that photo has become one of several iconic images that were captured on film during those pivotal days—moments of a national tragedy frozen in time—none of them standing alone tell the whole story.

On November 22, 1963, three shots were fired in Dallas, and the world stopped for four days. For an entire generation, it was the end of the age of innocence.

—*Clint Hill*

DAY ONE

———

NOVEMBER 21, 1963

TEXAS TRIP SCHEDULE

November 21st, (Thursday)

10:45 am	Leave W.H. by Helicopter
11:00 am	Leave Andrew AFB by jet
1:30 pm	Arrive Brooks AFB, San Antonio
1:40 pm	Motorcade through city
2:25 pm	Arrive Brooks AFB to dedicate Aero Space Medical Health Center
3:00 pm	Program ends, depart by car for Kelly AFB
3:30 pm	Departs Kelly AFB for Houston
4:15 pm	Arrive Houston International Airport motorcade through city
5:00 pm	Arrive Rice Hotel
	(tentative) drop by President's Club cocktail party in hotel
8:20 pm Speech ?	Drop by reception of Latin American Citizens in hotel
8:35 pm	Depart Hotel for Colloseum dinner for Congressman Thomas
8:45 pm	Arrive Colloseum
9:45 pm	Leave Colbseum for Airport
10:00 pm	Depart for Fort Worth
10:45 pm	Arrive Carswell AFB, Fort Worth leave by car for hotel
11:05 pm	Arrive Texas Hotel

November 22nd (Friday)

✓ 8:45 am	Chamber of Commerce Breakfast in Hotel
9:45 am	Breakfast ends Free period
10:45 am	Depart for Airport
11:15 am	Take off for Dallas
11:35 am	Arrive Dallas Love Field

- JBK won't attend -

November 22nd (continued)

11:45 am	Motorcade through Dallas
12:30 pm	Arrive Trade Mart for Luncheon
2:00 pm	Depart Trade Mart for Love Field
2:35 pm	Depart Love Field for Austin
3:15 pm	Arrive Bergstrom AFB Austin
3:25 pm	Depart by Car for town
3:55 pm	Arrive Commodore Perry Hotel (there will be a suite to rest in)
✓ 4:15-4:45 pm	Attend Reception in Hotel for Texas Congressional Delegation and State Executive Committee
	return to suite
6:00 pm	Arrive Governor's Mansion Reception for State Legislators
7:00 pm	Return to Hotel
8:30 pm	Depart Hotel for Colloseum and fund raising dinner
9:15 pm	Depart Colloseum for Airport
9:35 pm	Depart for LBJ Ranch

November 23rd (Saturday)

2:00 pm	Depart LBJ Ranch for Washington

✓ - JBK probably won't attend -

1

Leaving the White House

The day we left for Texas begins like countless other presidential trips. People hustling through the halls to get last-minute changes to speeches typed; secretaries and press staff clamoring to be added to the manifest of authorized personnel; the presidential staff and assistants coordinating all the details for the president and the first lady. Everyone wants to make sure this trip goes without a hitch. Not only because this unofficial start to the 1964 campaign is critically important politically, but also because First Lady Jacqueline Kennedy will be accompanying her husband on the three-day swing through the Lone Star State. Mrs. Kennedy prefers to stay out of politics and, in the three years of the administration thus far, never before has she traveled with the president on a domestic political trip. This is a first. As the Special Agent in Charge of Mrs. Kennedy's Secret Service Detail, it is my job to make sure nothing happens to her.

As with every trip the President of the United States takes, the schedule is planned to the minute. The political staff has designed the trip to maximize President Kennedy's exposure to the press and the general public, while simultaneously adding funds to the campaign coffer: grand Air Force One arrivals with plenty of pomp and circumstance; multiple motorcades through the main streets of each city; and breakfasts, luncheons, and dinners reserved for deep-pocketed donors.

Typical politics.

It was just yesterday that I returned to Washington with Mrs. Kennedy. She's spent the past several days riding her beloved horse, Sardar, at the Kennedys' newly finished residence near Middleburg, Virginia. After reviewing the typewritten schedule for the trip to Texas, she made some handwritten notes—both for her benefit and mine—about a couple of events she will not attend, and one in which she plans to make a short speech in Spanish. She uses her initials—JBK—for Jacqueline Bouvier Kennedy. This is typical of the way she and I operate. We have been together for three years, day in and day out, and have developed a trusting and comfortable relationship. While she prefers to be spontaneous, she knows I don't like surprises, and she knows that the more information she gives me in advance, the smoother things will go.

She also recognizes how important this trip is to her husband's reelection bid and she is eager to make a good impression. But when I see the rigorous schedule that's planned, I am concerned about her physical and emotional stamina.

It has been less than four months since Mrs. Kennedy gave birth to a baby boy—Patrick Bouvier Kennedy—who lived for just two days. The trauma of losing this son has taken its toll on both the president and Mrs. Kennedy. He, being President of the United States, has had no choice but to carry on—the world does not stop because of the death of a president's son. She, on the other hand, after spiraling into a deep depression, has finally started to return to her normal activities. The three-week cruise in the Mediterranean on the yacht *Christina,* back in October, helped her immensely, and I must admit, it was nice for me, too.

The death of Patrick was hard on all of us who are close to the family. And while the president and Mrs. Kennedy appear to be much closer since the tragedy—going so far as to hold hands in public—I know how stressful campaigning can be, and I certainly don't want anything to happen that might send her back to those dark days of depression. She's only just begun to smile again.

This morning, I arrive at the White House at eight o'clock, drop off my luggage with the transportation department in the West Wing basement, and head straight to my office. It isn't really an actual office, but a corner of the Map Room where I've set up a desk and a typewriter. Space in the White House is at a premium. Sitting at my desk, I have a clear view of the hallway and elevator that lead to the Kennedys' private residence.

Looking over Mrs. Kennedy's schedule, I realize there is a mistake. Her schedule indicates Air Force One will arrive at Brooks Air Force Base in San Antonio, while my schedule, which is far more detailed with Secret Service agents' assignments and hotel room numbers for everyone in the presidential party, indicates we land at San Antonio International Airport. I am almost certain that my schedule has the correct information, but to verify, I call Eve Dempsher. As the secretary to Jerry Behn, the Special Agent in Charge of the White House Secret Service Detail, Eve has every detail for the trip at her fingertips.

Sure enough, Eve says, we are landing at San Antonio International Airport. Whoever typed up Mrs. Kennedy's schedule made an error. It happens. But at least now I feel comfortable with the schedule.

The buzzer system sounds three times, indicating the president is moving throughout the residence, and moments later, President Kennedy walks out of the elevator. Seeing me through the doorway, he calls out, "Good morning, Clint."

"Good morning, Mr. President," I answer, as I snuff my cigarette into the already full ashtray on my desk.

The president strides toward my open door and says, "Clint, just so you know, John will be riding with us to Andrews."

"Yes, sir. I figured that might be the case. I'll make sure Agent Foster is aware." It has almost become routine for two-year-old John Jr. to ride along on the helicopter to Andrews Air Force Base whenever the president departs for a trip, and Agent Bob Foster is one of three agents on the Secret Service detail for the children—the Kiddie Detail. John loves helicopters. I mean, he really *loves* helicopters. Recently, Mrs. Kennedy told me she wouldn't be at all surprised if John becomes a pilot when he grows up. His excitement is contagious, and no one gets a bigger kick out of it than his father. Due to the demands of the job, President Kennedy's time with his son is often limited, and the short rides in the chopper together are precious.

President Kennedy's schedule is light this morning, with just one official meeting in the Oval Office—five minutes allotted for the U.S. ambassadors to the African republics of Upper Volta and Gabon. White House photographer Cecil Stoughton is summoned to take a photo as a memento for the guests, and a visual document of the meeting. Who could imagine that this mundane photo of President Kennedy

sitting so relaxed in his rocking chair, speaking with two ambassadors, would be the last image of him alive in the White House.

Meanwhile, upstairs, Providencia Paredes, Mrs. Kennedy's personal assistant, scurries around to make sure Mrs. Kennedy has everything she needs. Normally, Provi, as everyone calls her, would be traveling with Mrs. Kennedy, but this weekend Provi's son Gustavo is being confirmed into the Catholic Church. Not wanting Provi to miss such an important event, Mrs. Kennedy has asked her personal secretary, Mary Gallagher, to take Provi's place. President Kennedy's personal valet, George Thomas, will be in charge of the president's clothing and belongings, and he, too, will be part of the entourage.

Being Thursday, it is a school day, so Caroline—who will turn six on November 27—has already said good-bye to her parents, and is settled into her normal routine with classmates in the small, private White House school on the third floor.

At around 10:40 A.M., the sound of the helicopter arriving on the South Lawn is the signal that it's departure time. I slip the schedule into my briefcase, double-check my suit coat pockets to make sure I've got everything—sunglasses, wallet, and the leather bifold commission book that proves I'm a Special Agent in the United States Secret Service, "worthy of trust and confidence"—and stuff my .38-caliber snub-nosed revolver into the holster on my hip.

It is a select few who ride as passengers on the presidential helicopter—the president, Mrs. Kennedy, and John; top staff members like Ken O'Donnell, Dave Powers, and Evelyn Lincoln; a military aide; Roy Kellerman, the Assistant Special Agent in Charge of the White House Detail; myself; and Agent Bob Foster, who will accompany young John on the short flight, and then return with him to the White House when the rest of us transfer to Air Force One.

At exactly 10:50 A.M. we lift off the White House grounds and the trip to Texas begins.

John sits by the window, wriggly and animated, with a constant grin on his face throughout the entire six-minute flight. When the chopper lands gently on the tarmac alongside the presidential plane, however, his whole demeanor changes. He has been told he can't go on the trip with Mummy and Daddy, and suddenly it hits him that now it's time to say good-bye.

"Good-bye, John," President Kennedy says as he gives John a hug.

"Can't I come?" John begs with quivering lips, tears welling in his eyes. "I want to come."

Mrs. Kennedy holds him close and says, "It's just a few days, John. And when we come back, it will be your birthday." On November 25, John will turn three years old. Both children have birthdays coming up in the busy week ahead.

But the promise of a birthday party does nothing to appease John. I feel sorry for him, and it hits me, too, because earlier this morning I said good-bye to my own two sons, Chris and Corey, who are nearly the same ages as John and Caroline. My job requires me to be with Mrs. Kennedy wherever she goes, and for the past three years that has meant I've spent more time with Caroline and John than with my own sons.

Finally, despite the tears, we can delay no longer. The president gives his son one last hug and starts for the door of the chopper. He turns and looks at Agent Foster, who has slid into the seat next to John, and says something I will never forget.

"Take care of John for me, won't you, Mr. Foster?"

I've witnessed many tearful good-byes between the president and his children, but he's never said anything like this before.

"Yes, sir, Mr. President," Foster replies. "I'll be glad to do that."

As I follow Mrs. Kennedy out of the chopper, I turn to John and, trying to sound as cheerful as possible, I say, "Bye-bye, John. You have fun with Mr. Foster, now, okay? We'll be back in a few days."

His sobs grow louder and louder as we walk toward the portable staircase leading to Air Force One. After all they've been through, I know John's cries tug at President and Mrs. Kennedy's hearts. Just before they enter the door of the plane, they each turn to their son, and wave.

2

Air Force One

The three-hour-and-twenty-five-minute flight to San Antonio is relaxing and pleasant. I have never lost sight of the rare privilege it is to travel aboard the presidential aircraft. Air Force One—a customized Boeing 707 with tail number 26000—is configured to accommodate the president as if he were in the White House, complete with a state-of-the-art communications system that can connect to any telephone in the world. The presidential stateroom in the center portion of the plane contains an office with a desk, table, and sofa, and an adjacent bedroom with bathroom, giving the president a private area to work, rest, or have conferences with staff. About a third of the plane is set up with first-class-type airline seats, which are used by the press, staff, and Secret Service. This particular plane has been in service only since the spring of 1962, and few people know that Mrs. Kennedy herself had a hand in designing the elegant interior as well as changing the exterior color scheme. The previous jets were painted a garish orange, while the new ones have a sleek silver, white, and blue theme with the presidential seal and UNITED STATES OF AMERICA painted boldly on the side. This same design will remain on all presidential jets for decades to come.

There are a total of nine Secret Service agents aboard, including Assistant Special Agent in Charge Roy Kellerman and myself. Kellerman and I sit together, going over the plans and intermittently dozing off. President Kennedy spends most of the time in the office area with his three closest advisors, Larry O'Brien, Ken O'Donnell, and Dave Powers—fondly yet facetiously known as "the Irish Mafia." He's very relaxed, wandering through the aircraft at times, greeting those on board. The Air Force One radio operator is constantly sending and receiving messages. He is always the busiest person on board. Mrs. Kennedy sits for a while with her press secretary, Pam Turnure, going over the schedule and plans for the rest of the year's activities: a birthday party for John on Monday; Caroline's birthday party on Wednesday; Thanksgiving up at Hyannis Port, Massachusetts; Christmas in Palm Beach, Florida.

The president and his staff wanted this trip to Texas to appear nonpolitical, but clearly it is all about politics. The Kennedy-Johnson ticket won in 1960 by the slimmest of margins. Some alleged fraud. They carried the state of Texas by a mere forty-one thousand votes—not a very wide margin considering it was Lyndon Johnson's home state. In order to ensure their reelection in 1964, they realize they must increase the electoral vote count, and two states are critical: Florida and Texas. Their position on civil rights continues to be a problem throughout the South, and that needs to be addressed. Additionally, in Texas, the Democratic Party is in a shambles, due to the fact that Governor John Connally and the senior senator, Ralph Yarborough, can't stand each other. The bickering and fighting has created such a divide in the state Democratic Party that it threatens to undermine the solidarity required for the presidential election. President Kennedy and Vice President Johnson need to tend to the political wounds within the various factions and find a way to show a united face that represents all the party members within the state. This is the real reason for the trip to Texas.

At one point during the flight, I hear Mrs. Kennedy speaking in Spanish. On the Houston stop, the president intends to drop in on a dinner sponsored by the League of United Latin American Citizens (LULAC) and he suggested that Mrs. Kennedy make a short address in Spanish. She is fluent in French and Spanish, and on several international trips, her language skills were the equivalent of political gold. In France she was able to charm the aloof Charles de Gaulle into allowing the *Mona Lisa* to be exhibited throughout the United States. In Mexico, Venezuela, and Puerto Rico her ability to connect with leaders on a personal level had gone a long way in helping the president pass his Alliance for Progress program.

In 1960, Hispanics were just 3 percent of the general population in the United States, but they voted overwhelmingly for Kennedy-Johnson. In Texas, Kennedy and Johnson won 91 percent of the Hispanic vote. President Kennedy realizes the small but growing Latino population in America might very well be key to his reelection in certain states, and especially in Texas.

Mrs. Kennedy practices her lines over and over. She doesn't want to make a mistake, and above all, she wants to make her husband proud.

The Air Force One stewards serve a light lunch to everyone aboard, while Kellerman and I go over the detailed reports that outline the duties and post assignments of the Secret Service agents. Trips like this are always quite stressful for the agents involved. We have a schedule and a plan to follow, but when dealing in the political world, everything is subject to change, and oftentimes does. We must be adaptable and capable of changing plans on a moment's notice. The only relaxing parts of this entire trip will be when we are aboard Air Force One.

We are on final approach to San Antonio International Airport. The adrenaline in my body begins to rise as I anticipate what lies ahead. The staff seems to have very high expectations for a successful trip. Packed-house fund-raising events interspersed with highly publicized public speeches and strategically planned motorcade routes are expected to draw large crowds—large crowds with unknown attitudes. Will they be friendly or hostile? We have no intelligence information to indicate a problem here in San Antonio; however, one never knows exactly what will take place. It is that "unknown" that, from the moment we hit the ground, keeps the agents on edge.

3

San Antonio Arrival

We land at 1:30 P.M. Central Standard Time. The staff is giddy, all smiles, while we, the agents, put our game faces on. It's showtime.

As pilot Colonel James Swindal glides Air Force One to its designated parking spot, there is a roar of hollers and whistles. Nearly five thousand people have come to San Antonio International Airport to catch a glimpse of President and Mrs. Kennedy.

Standard protocol calls for the president to be the first to emerge from the aircraft, but moments before the door opens, President Kennedy says, "Jackie, you go first." Grinning, he adds, "Most of these people have come to see you."

He is right. We have seen it all around the world—the crowds automatically double whenever Mrs. Kennedy accompanies the president. And as soon as Mrs. Kennedy begins to descend the steps, a group of schoolchildren on the upper deck of the terminal start chanting, "Jackie! Jackie! Jackie!"

Smiling broadly, she acknowledges them with a wave as President Kennedy eases down the steps behind her, clearly elated, and perhaps a bit surprised, with the enthusiastic welcome. Agent Kellerman and I move quickly down the steps after them, scanning the surrounding area as we descend.

"Look up there," I say to Kellerman, pointing to the roof of the terminal, where people of all ages, including small children, are packed onto the open-air rooftop observation deck, screaming, waving, and clapping. "There must be a thousand people up there."

Hundreds more are jammed inside the airport terminal, their faces pressed against the glass windows.

Political trips tend to have very repetitive scenes. Airport arrivals, greeting committees made up of local political figures and officials, shaking hands with crowds of people, motorcades strategically positioned to move through heavily populated downtown areas for maximum exposure, carefully chosen speech sites, head tables with coveted seating positions for deep-pocketed donors and campaigning politicians, hotel arrivals, and, finally, airport departures, which start the routine all over again with another arrival in another city. On this trip, the Democratic governor of Texas, John Connally, and his wife, Nellie, are the official hosts, and, from this point on, Governor and Mrs. Connally will accompany the Kennedys each and every step of the way.

Vice President and Mrs. Johnson will be sort of secondary hosts, and while they

will also attend every function, they will travel on the vice presidential plane, known as Air Force Two. They'll fly to each destination a few minutes ahead of the president, be there when Air Force One lands, and be part of the welcoming committee at every stop. Here in San Antonio, the official welcoming committee consists of the Connallys, the Johnsons, the mayor of San Antonio and his wife, a contingent of congressmen, other local politicians, and a select group of schoolchildren and Boy Scouts.

Dennis Halterman, the Secret Service agent who was sent ahead to do the advance security arrangements, is our man on the ground. He knows the route, the venues, and has arranged the minute details of security. Everybody allowed on the tarmac has been cleared by Halterman, the local Secret Service office, and the local police officers, but still, you never really know who is in a crowd like this. It is 1963 and there are no magnetometers, no video camera surveillance, no personal communication devices. The nine agents who were aboard Air Force One create an envelope of security around President and Mrs. Kennedy, using hand signals and eye contact to notify each other of individuals in the crowd who give us any measure of concern. Fortunately, the fencing and strong enforcement by the local police officers keep the enthusiastic general public contained and far enough away that President Kennedy is deterred from heading into the screaming mass.

After shaking a few hands among the screened guests, President and Mrs. Kennedy proceed to the presidential limousine, which, along with the Secret Service follow-up car, was flown ahead to San Antonio on a C-130 cargo plane. This is exactly the way we, the agents, prefer arrivals to be managed—limited crowd access and quick movement into the waiting vehicles to get the motorcade under way.

4

San Antonio Motorcade

The 1961 midnight-blue Lincoln Continental presidential limousine—which the Secret Service calls "SS-100-X"—was designed especially for use in parade-type situations just like this. The standard four-door convertible had been lengthened three and a half feet and was equipped with various configurations of removable tops. There is a hard top, a canvas roof panel, and a transparent Plexiglas bubble top—all of which are stackable and can be stored in the trunk. Contrary to popular belief, the presidential vehicle is not armored, and none of the roofs have bullet-resistant properties. Since the purpose of a showy presidential motorcade is to allow the people to see the president up close, President Kennedy always insists on having the tops off whenever possible. The only times we use the bubble top or the hard top are when there is inclement weather, or if it's so windy that Mrs. Kennedy's hair might blow too much. This is standard procedure.

The tops are attached to a wide metal bar that runs above and behind the front bench seat. The rear compartment contains a rear bench seat, which is always reserved for the president. In between the rear and forward benches are two jump seats—specifically for additional guests of the president—which fold forward when not occupied. When the jump seats are in use, the legroom for all the passengers is restricted.

There is a protocol for presidential motorcades, which dictates the order of the vehicles in the procession and the seating positions of the passengers in the presidential limousine. The president always sits in the right rear, the first lady in the left rear. Guests ride in the jump seats.

Unfortunately, no one has briefed Nellie Connally on the proper protocol. With the handshaking completed on the tarmac, Mrs. Connally steps into the back of the limousine and sits on the left side of the rear bench. No one wants to point out her mistake, so Mrs. Kennedy simply gets in and sits down next to her, leaving the right rear position for President Kennedy, while Governor Connally sits in the left jump seat. The press is having a field day, and people are snapping photos all over the place. Even one of the stewardesses from the press plane pulls out her camera, eager to get a close-up of the glamorous foursome in the limousine. Now that everyone is situated, the motorcade gets under way.

The Secret Service has standard operating procedures for motorcades with assigned positions for all the vehicles. There are marked and unmarked police cars, police motorcycles, cars or buses for press and VIPs, as well as the presidential limousine and the Secret Service follow-up car. On this trip to Texas, however, because the vice president is traveling in the motorcades with the president—a rare and unusual situation—we have the addition of the vice president's car and his Secret Service follow-up car.

The crowd on the rooftop erupts into a cheer as we exit the airport and head down Broadway, the main thoroughfare through San Antonio, toward our destination of Brooks Air Force Base. Typically, city streets are chosen over highways whenever possible when the purpose is for the people to be able to see the president. The route was published in the newspapers and the people have come out by the thousands, just to get a chance to see President and Mrs. Kennedy drive by. The president's visit is such a rare occasion that local schools have declared today a holiday. The crowds are large and boisterous, friendly and exuberant.

As the motorcade proceeds through the city, the follow-up car maintains a distance of about five feet behind the presidential limousine at all times. Agent Bill Greer, the driver of the president's car, and Agent Sam Kinney, the driver of the follow-up car, are well trained and have driven in motorcades all over the world. They know the cars, how they handle, and they've done this so many times, it's almost like there's a consistently taut invisible rope between the two vehicles. When Greer speeds up or slows down, Kinney immediately changes speed to adjust.

We are on a tight time schedule, and the motorcade is moving along around twenty-five miles per hour. At this speed, the agents stand on the running boards of the follow-up car, also known as "Halfback." The running boards provide an elevated position for us to observe the crowds and provide easy access to be able to jump off toward the presidential limousine when necessary.

Up ahead a group of cadets from Texas Military Institute are waving a big banner. President Kennedy sees them and says, "Slow down, Bill," to the driver. Bill Greer slows down, almost to a stop, and the cadets rush forward to shake the president's hand. He smiles, reaches out his hand and commends the young men on their military endeavors, and we move on.

Suddenly, a group of women surge toward the president from the right-hand side of the road.

"Mr. President! Mr. President!" they shriek. "Let me shake your hand!"

"Slow down, Bill," President Kennedy says again. He doesn't want to disappoint them—these are voters, after all. Greer slows down, and it's as if it's an invitation for the throngs of people on all sides to charge toward the car.

All the agents leap off the running boards and surround the president's limousine to keep the surging crowd away. Our job is to form an envelope of protection around President and Mrs. Kennedy—literally, a human shield. The president stands up and, grinning widely, reaches out to shake as many of the women's hands as possible. Some of them shriek and carry on like he's handing out hundred-dollar bills.

Mrs. Kennedy remains seated, but smiling, far less comfortable than the president in this circuslike atmosphere.

Apparently there has been some conversation in the presidential car about the seating arrangements. It looks strange to have three people in the back and one in the middle in the jump seat. So it's decided that Mrs. Connally should move to the jump seat next to Governor Connally. The car comes to a complete stop and the crowd goes absolutely crazy.

We have no choice but to push people back and try to get their attention with authority.

"Get back! Get back!"

The president continues waving and shaking hands as Governor Connally and

the two women switch their seats. Once everyone is seated, the motorcade gets under way again.

As we enter the business district, it feels like Mardi Gras in New Orleans. We are driving through a mass of humanity. The sidewalks are jammed so that people are spilling into the street on both sides of the motorcade—children on fathers' shoulders; teenagers jumping up and down; screaming women in pillbox hats and "Jackie-style" suits. That is just the street level. As we turn from Houston Street onto St. Mary's, past the Gunter Hotel, people are packed onto balconies, hanging out windows, standing on rooftops and fire escapes.

President and Mrs. Kennedy and Governor and Mrs. Connally are enjoying every minute—laughing, waving. It is exactly what the political people want and makes for great photo opportunities. For the Secret Service, the slow pace and the unscreened people above and around us are exactly what we do not want. Sunglasses hide our eyes as we scan the crowd, looking at hands and eyes. Amid the adulation, we are searching for the glimmer of a gun, or the lone person who is not reacting like the others, but instead has a crazed look in his eyes as his hand reaches into his pocket. This is as tense as it gets.

After another couple of miles, it seems the wind picks up and Mrs. Kennedy's hair is really blowing. Another discussion, another stop. Hold back the crowds as Mrs. Kennedy changes places with Governor Connally. Now the two women are in the jump seats, with the governor and the president seated side by side on the rear bench seat.

It's like musical chairs, and all these stops create anxiety for the Secret Service as well as the local police, who are trying to keep us on the planned timetable.

We are fifteen minutes behind schedule and need to make up some time, so the motorcade speed increases. Now, for the duration of the motorcade, along with "Jackie!" and "Yay JFK!" we hear "Slow down! Slow down!"

The next day the newspapers will be filled with complaints from people along the motorcade who say they barely got a glimpse because the cars were going so fast.

"I was so mad I could cry," lamented one female spectator. "I wanted to get a picture but they went by so fast I just snapped a picture and I don't know what I got if anything." Her sentiments were echoed by others who thought if the president and first lady took the trouble to go through the city they at least should have gone slowly enough to see them.

5

Brooks Air Force Base

At 2:40 P.M. we pull up to the Aerospace Medical Center at Brooks Air Force Base, where the commander of the Aerospace Medical Division is waiting to greet President and Mrs. Kennedy. We walk briskly through the building, and as we exit the doors, we find a raised stage overlooking a vast expanse of grassy field, on which nine thousand folding chairs have been set up—each one of them filled—with thousands more standing on the outskirts. The crowd is a mix of civilians in their Sunday best and Air Force personnel in their dress blues, and as soon as the president emerges from the door, they stand up in unison, clapping, as the band plays ruffles and flourishes and "Hail to the Chief."

It is a warm afternoon, and the sun is blazing overhead. Ladies in the crowd fan themselves with the program, or use it to shield their eyes from the sun. The president is here to dedicate four new structures of the Aerospace Medical Division. With just thirty-five minutes allotted on the schedule, the introduction is brief and the president moves to the podium to address the crowd.

For more than three years, I have spoken to the American people in terms of the New Frontier. That is not a partisan term. It is not the exclusive property of Republicans or Democrats. It refers instead to this nation's place in history—to the fact that we do stand on the edge of a great new era, filled

27

with both crisis and opportunities, an era to be characterized by achievements and by challenges.

It is an era which calls for action, and for the best efforts of all who are willing to explore the unknown and test the uncertain, in every phase of human endeavor. It is a time for pathfinders and pioneers.

I have come to Texas today to salute an outstanding group of pioneers— the men who man the Brooks Air Force Base School of Aerospace Medicine and the Aerospace Medical Center.

The people are rapt with attention, hanging on his every word. He is a gifted speaker, and every word is uttered with conviction and passion. He refers to his visit

to Cape Canaveral last Saturday, during which he saw the new Saturn C1 rocket booster, which will put the United States at the forefront of space exploration.

He ends the short speech with a reference to literature, as he so often does.

> *Frank O'Connor, the Irish writer, tells in one of his books how, as a boy, he and his friends would make their way across the countryside; and when they came to an orchard wall that seemed too high to climb, too doubtful to try, too difficult to permit their journey to continue, they took off their caps and tossed them over the wall—and then they had no choice but to follow them.*
>
> *My friends, this nation has tossed its cap over the wall of space—and we have no choice but to follow it. Whatever the difficulties, they must be overcome. Whatever the hazards, they must be guarded against. With the vital help of this Aerospace Medical Center, with the help of all who labor in this space endeavor, with the help and support of all Americans, we will climb this wall with safety and with speed—and we shall then explore the wonders on the other side.*

The people love it. They love him. All nine thousand people bolt out of their seats in unison with a standing ovation and deafening applause. Their response is like a magnet—enticing President Kennedy to them. He grabs Mrs. Kennedy's hand and leads her toward the crowd.

As Agent Kellerman and I make eye contact, acknowledging we are each aware of the situation, President Kennedy says something quietly in Mrs. Kennedy's ear, which causes her to break into laughter. They are having a wonderful time together, high on the elixir of the crowd's adulation.

During the 1960 campaign, Mrs. Kennedy was pregnant with John and thus did very little campaigning with her husband. In the three years since, the couple's popularity has grown to the point that they are idolized like movie stars. To see them appear together in a public situation like this is such a rare occurrence that the people who are in proximity realize this is a once-in-a-lifetime opportunity. Even in this rather staid crowd of military personnel, people are pushing and shoving to get as

close as possible to the Kennedys as they can. It is a politician's ideal situation and a Secret Service agent's nightmare. Like oil and water, politics and protection just don't mix.

President Kennedy thrives on this dizzying atmosphere and dives into the crowd, shaking as many hands as possible. Having become so close to Mrs. Kennedy, I know she is really very shy, and this kind of situation is not one she enjoys. But she has promised her husband she will support him however she can in this reelection campaign. She looks to me for reassurance before following the president's lead. I am within inches of her, ready to intervene if necessary, as she timidly offers her hand to the screaming mass.

Suddenly a glassy-eyed woman breaks through the crowd and lunges at Mrs. Kennedy.

"Mrs. Kennedy! Mrs. Kennedy, please touch my hand!"

She grabs at one of Mrs. Kennedy's white-gloved hands and shrieks, "Oh my God! She touched me! She really did!"

The woman is harmless, but I can see the fearful look on Mrs. Kennedy's face. I immediately put my hand firmly on the small of her back and push her beyond the woman's reach.

After several minutes of shaking hands, the president waves to the crowd and turns back toward the building. En masse, the crowd groans a sigh of dismay.

"Clint," Agent Kellerman says, "the base commander invited the president to see some men in a space simulator, some sort of oxygen chamber. It's not on the schedule but the president wants to go."

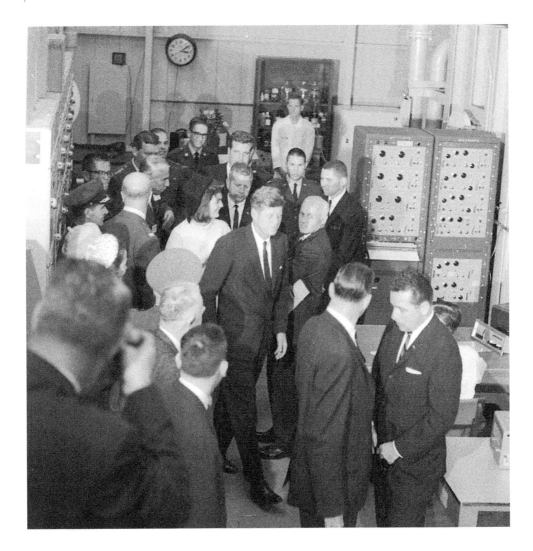

It makes sense. The space program is one of President Kennedy's prime interests.

Four airmen are inside a space cabin simulator, breathing pure oxygen at a simulated altitude of 27,500 feet.

"They've been in there since November third," the commander explains, handing President Kennedy a headset with microphone so he can talk to them. "And they've got seventeen more days to go."

Captivated and intrigued, President Kennedy fires a series of questions at the young men.

"How do you feel? Where do you sleep? Any problems? What do you hope to learn?"

He's clearly impressed with the experiment. Taking off the headset, he offers it to Mrs. Kennedy.

"Here, Jackie, have a talk with the men."

Conscious of the beret so carefully clipped to her hair, she declines the headset but waves at the men, smiling with admiration.

President Kennedy turns to one of the scientists leading the program and asks, "Do you think your work here might have medical applications apart from space research? Is it possible your work might help improve oxygen chambers for premature babies?"

The scientist agrees that it very well might.

President Kennedy looks at his wife, and their eyes lock. Nothing is said, but I know they are both thinking about their baby Patrick—his recent birth and death still so fresh in all our minds. The clock is ticking, however, and now we are even further behind schedule. President and Mrs. Kennedy thank their hosts and the entourage walks briskly to the waiting vehicles. Mrs. Kennedy settles into the rear bench seat on the left side of SS-100-X, the president is on her right, and Governor and Mrs. Connally fold down the jump seats just in front of them. Standard protocol seating seems to have finally stuck.

Hundreds of people have moved from the other side of the building, hoping to see the Kennedys as they depart, and once again we agents are on high alert. I move into position so I'm standing next to Mrs. Kennedy, my right hand on the car. As driver Bill Greer slowly accelerates, I walk alongside, then break into a jog, staying as close to Mrs. Kennedy as possible, constantly scanning the crowd.

The president is thrilled with the enthusiastic welcome San Antonio has given them.

"That was really something—those men in that oxygen chamber," he remarks to Governor Connally. Connally beams. Other than the slight delay in schedule, everything is going remarkably well.

Mrs. Kennedy is pensive, but much more relaxed now that she's in the safety of the limousine. As Bill Greer speeds up, I drop back to the follow-up car, reach for the handhold, and jump onto the left running board position next to driver Sam Kinney.

Our destination is Kelly Air Force Base, and while the crowds along this stretch are not as dense as those in the downtown business section of San Antonio, I'm amazed at how many people there are all along the way.

6

Kelly Air Force Base

Three hundred San Antonio police officers have assisted us with security, and as we arrive at Kelly Air Force Base, several officers are standing at attention. President Kennedy requests Greer to stop. Agent Kellerman jumps out and opens the door for President Kennedy, who walks over to the officers.

Reaching out his hand to one of them, the president says, "I want to thank you and your fellow officers for the fine job you've done this afternoon."

The police officer seems to be in complete shock as he shakes the president's hand. It is a moment he will never forget.

We drive onto the base, and although we will be here for just a few minutes, five thousand people are waiting to greet us. Young officers are sitting on others' shoulders to get a better view. Wives, girlfriends, sons, and daughters have joined the servicemen, and as the motorcade comes to a stop, the people clap and shriek. A row of Air Force policemen keeps the crowd contained as President and Mrs. Kennedy reach into the crowd to shake hands.

The three aircraft that brought the presidential entourage to Texas—Air Force One; the backup plane with tail number 86970, which will now serve as the vice president's plane; and the Pan Am chartered press plane—were flown from San Antonio International Airport here to Kelly Air Force Base while we were motorcading through the city. Why? Pure politics. Rather than have the motorcade double back to San Antonio Airport after visiting Brooks Aerospace Medical Center, and pass by the same people who had just seen them, transferring the planes to a new departure point provides the opportunity for more people to see the president.

At 4:00 P.M. we are wheels up, headed for Houston. Air Force One takes off first, followed a few minutes later by the vice president's plane and the Pan Am press plane. We are thirty minutes behind schedule, but everyone aboard Air Force One is elated. In two and a half hours on the ground, President and Mrs. Kennedy appeared before an estimated 125,000 citizens. The hope is that this personal contact will leave a lasting, positive impression that ultimately puts Kennedy and Johnson back in the White House in 1964.

7

Houston Airport Arrival

T he flight from San Antonio to Houston covers less than two hundred miles and takes just thirty-five minutes. The president's Secret Service detail has changed shifts, so the agents aboard Air Force One are different from those who were on the Washington–San Antonio flight, due to the time of day and a change of shifts. Previously, the 8:00–4:00 shift was on duty; now the 4:00–midnight shift will accompany the president. The midnight–8:00 shift will take over in Fort Worth. Each shift has just five agents, plus Kellerman as the agent in charge, and the drivers. For the protection of Mrs. Kennedy, there are just two of us—Agent Paul Landis and myself.

During the flight, Kellerman and I review the survey report submitted by the Secret Service advance agent, to get some idea of what to expect on arrival. The large parade-type vehicles we used in San Antonio—SS-100-X and the Secret Service follow-up car—are being flown ahead to Dallas for use tomorrow. Unfortunately, the Secret Service does not have enough vehicles to be able to provide them at each location, so in Houston we will use leased vehicles—a standard four-door Lincoln convertible for the presidential party and a Mercury convertible for the follow-up car. It's a far less desirable situation for the president and the Secret Service, but when you're hopping from city to city all in one day, there's no other choice.

The press plane lands ten minutes ahead of Air Force One—just enough time for the reporters and photographers to get into position—followed a few minutes later by the vice president's plane. Vice President and Mrs. Johnson move into position with the local dignitaries who are already lined up, ready to greet President and Mrs. Kennedy—as if they hadn't just seen them half an hour before in San Antonio. This is politics.

As I exit the aircraft behind President and Mrs. Kennedy, I am struck by two things. First, the heat. While the wind is blowing, it does nothing to cool the air, nor diminish the brightness of the blazing sun, low on the horizon. The second thing that grabs my attention is the carnival-like atmosphere emanating from the massive crowd gathered behind a fence line on the tarmac. There must be eight thousand people—men and women, young and old, families with children, Boy Scout troops and college students—screaming, whooping, waving small American flags, holding up signs and banners.

A band begins to play ruffles and flourishes, but even the trumpets can't drown out the screeches.

"Mr. President! Jackieeee! Welcome to Houston! Pleeease, come over here!"

Once again Mrs. Kennedy is first down the ramp, and at the bottom Vice President Johnson introduces her to the mayor and his wife, who hands Mrs. Kennedy a huge bouquet of yellow roses. Mrs. Kennedy accepts the flowers graciously, despite the fact that now she must juggle them with her purse. Clutching her purse in her left hand, she cradles the bouquet, thorns and all, in her left arm like an infant, in order to keep her right hand free for the obligatory handshaking down the rest of the receiving line.

As the president and Mrs. Kennedy near the end of the line, the noise level of the crowd increases dramatically.

"Please, Mr. President! Come over here! We want to see Jackie!"

President Kennedy needs no further invitation, and when he begins walking toward the crowd, his wife dutifully following, the assembled throng reacts with frenzy. Fathers hoist children onto shoulders, urging the bewildered youngsters to reach out their hands. Cameras flash, women shriek. As the president and Mrs. Kennedy walk along the edge of the screaming mass, smiling, touching as many hands as possible, we, the agents, stick as close as possible, trying not to interfere but wishing

to God they'd finish this up and get into the cars. It's the kind of situation that, in a split second, can so easily get out of control.

Finally the president decides he has done enough politicking. He waves to the crowd, reaches for his wife's elbow, and they head toward the four-door Lincoln Continental convertible that will serve as the presidential vehicle in Houston. The standard configuration of the car requires Mrs. Connally to ride in the front seat between driver Bill Greer and Agent Kellerman, while Governor Connally, Mrs. Kennedy, and the president squeeze into the backseat. It is very crowded—and not nearly as impressive as SS-100-X.

At 4:50 P.M., twenty-five minutes behind schedule, the motorcade departs as the crowd continues to cheer and clap, the flags waving in the breeze. I, along with the other agents assigned to the follow-up car, walk alongside the presidential vehicle, constantly scanning the crowd, until the driver picks up speed and we drop back to the follow-up car.

The two-door Mercury convertible we are using as a follow-up car does not have running boards like "Halfback," which makes it awkward for us to ride in such a way that we can easily jump off when necessary. Each of us, in our own style—some not very gracefully—mount the sides of the car, either riding sort of sidesaddle, or in a straddling position, one leg inside the car and one leg outside. It is very uncomfortable, and I'm hoping we can breeze into the downtown area to the Rice Hotel as quickly as possible.

But details of the motorcade route were spelled out in the local newspapers this morning, and the crowds here are just as big as the ones in San Antonio. Even along the Gulf Freeway there are people standing on the shoulders of the road, and as we drive by, they surge toward us. Traffic in the other direction has come to a complete stop. It's off the car and on again. Off and on, as we crawl toward the city's skyline. All of us are dripping with sweat, as we spend more time jogging alongside the president's car than riding. The sun is setting fast, and there is notable disappointment from the people lined up ten and twenty deep along Travis Street who have waited for hours but can now barely see President and Mrs. Kennedy as darkness falls.

8

Rice Hotel

Forty minutes after departing the airport, we finally arrive at the Rice Hotel. Police are having difficulty holding back the crowd gathered on the opposite side of the street. As soon as the presidential car pulls to a stop, all you can hear are shrieks and screams.

"Welcome to Houston, Jackie!" "We love you, Mr. President!" "Please, look over here!"

Naturally, the president acquiesces, and urges Mrs. Kennedy to join him. People claw to touch them, and once again they try to touch as many people as possible. But they are both windblown and withered, like the limp bouquet of yellow roses Mrs. Kennedy still cradles in her arms because she is too considerate to simply leave them in the backseat of the car. Finally, we get them to the hotel entrance, hoping for some space, but it is not to be.

The hotel lobby is jammed. People are everywhere, swarming, craving for a glimpse of the first couple, pushing and reaching for one moment of contact. I will never understand what drives people to behave like this. All I can do is stay close to Mrs. Kennedy, as her last line of defense.

Finally, with the help of the hotel manager, we get them into the elevator and up to the fifth floor to the four-room International Suite. Their luggage has been delivered, and they have three hours to relax, eat a small meal, and change clothes in preparation for the dinner in recognition of Senator Albert Thomas at the Houston Coliseum.

The event was originally to have taken place here at the Rice Hotel, but so many tickets were sold—more than 3,300—that at the last minute it had to be moved to the larger venue.

Agent Paul Landis and I are assigned to Room 525, next door to President and Mrs. Kennedy, but we barely use it. There just isn't time to transport baggage for the entire party, so although our shirts and suits are soiled with dirt and sweat, the best we can do is wash our faces and hands. This is but a pit stop, and we still have several more movements before the night is over.

The agents from the day shift—8:00 A.M.–4:00 P.M.—are en route to the Houston Coliseum to secure the venue for this evening's activities. They've been providing security at the Rice Hotel until our arrival, and now the current shift, the 4:00 P.M.–midnight shift, takes over. The number of agents is so small, a constant juggling act is required to adequately secure the venues and protect the president and Mrs. Kennedy at each location. The day and evening shifts will both work at least several hours of overtime, and for Landis, Kellerman, and me, it will be a sixteen- to eighteen-hour day.

At 8:40 P.M., President and Mrs. Kennedy emerge from their suite. They have both changed clothes—the president is wearing a fresh shirt, suit, and tie, and Mrs. Kennedy has put on an elegant black cut-velvet dress with a three-strand pearl necklace. As Agent Kellerman and I escort them down to the second-floor ballroom, hotel employees stand at attention along the hallway, breaking into huge smiles when the president and first lady oblige their outstretched hands with fleeting handshakes.

The brief appearance at the Latin American group has, of course, been planned all along, the security tightly coordinated, but it's designed to appear as an impromptu visit. When President and Mrs. Kennedy walk through the doors of the grand ballroom, the shock from the seven hundred guests is palpable.

Hoots and hollers, cheering and clapping, are accompanied by gasps of disbelief. The president makes his way to the stage, smiling with delight at the overwhelming welcome, and steps up to the podium. He speaks for a few minutes about the important relationship between the United States and the Latin American countries, and then offers the crowd a surprise.

"Well, I'm glad to be here today," he says. "And in order that, uh, my words can be even clearer, I'm going to ask my wife to say a few words to you also."

Applause and cheers reverberate off the walls as Mrs. Kennedy makes her way to the podium. Smiling shyly—she's not used to being in the spotlight like this—she takes her place at the podium and delivers her memorized speech in Spanish, stumbling just once over one word, but is otherwise flawless. She speaks for just thirty-five

seconds, but that is enough for this crowd, and instantaneously everyone is on their feet, cheering as if this were the most eloquent, inspiring speech they've ever heard.

"Viva Jackie! Viva JFK!"

President Kennedy is beaming, and as he and Mrs. Kennedy exchange glances, the adoration they have for each other is evident. He couldn't be more proud, and she is so pleased with the reaction from the people. Vice President Johnson steps up to the podium, grinning as big as can be—for the first lady's Spanish-speaking ability

reflects well on him, too—and acknowledges that whatever he has to say will be very insignificant in light of what Mrs. Kennedy has said.

The mariachi band behind them breaks into a rousing number, and while the schedule calls for us to depart immediately, the president, Mrs. Kennedy, and Vice President and Mrs. Johnson stay a while longer to shake hands and sign the group's guest book.

You can feel the joy and pride from every single person in this room, for it is the first time the Latin American community has been formally and personally acknowledged by a president of the United States.

9

Houston Coliseum

Congressman Albert Thomas Dinner

At 8:55 P.M. the presidential party piles into the cars again for the short drive to the Sam Houston Coliseum. It is dark, making it difficult to see the passengers inside, but still, curious crowds line the streets, people straining to catch a view of their president and first lady. Driving in open-top cars, in the dark, makes for a tense situation for the Secret Service.

I'm straddling the left-side door, and up ahead, as we approach the Coliseum, a group of protestors begins chanting, waving placards denouncing President Kennedy's policy—or lack thereof—with regard to Cuba. The demonstrators appear nonviolent, but we are mindful of how quickly attitudes can change, especially with dissenting groups. We've seen it plenty of times before—all it takes is one instigator to turn a manageable crowd into sheer chaos. Glaring at the picketers, I move to a sidesaddle position, freeing both my arms, and ready to jump in a split second. The chants continue as we come to a stop in front of the Coliseum, and we whisk the president and Mrs. Kennedy inside.

The sold-out event is a tribute to Congressman Albert Thomas, who has served his district for more than thirty years and is credited with bringing the Manned

Spacecraft Center to Houston. The dinner, attended by supporters of Congressman Thomas, is an opportunity for President Kennedy to bring together the various factions within the Democratic Party in Texas in time for the 1964 presidential election.

When President Kennedy steps up to the podium, no one in the audience could guess what a grueling day he's had to this point, for he appears completely relaxed, even energized by the enthusiastic reception he has received here and in San Antonio. He speaks glowingly of Congressman Thomas and of the space program, which is so important not only to him but to this local audience.

"Next month, when the United States of America fires the largest booster in the history of the world into space, for the first time giving us the lead—fires the largest payroll"—he realizes that's not the word he meant to say, and immediately corrects himself—"*payload* into space, giving us the lead." His mind is so quick that he turns this slight gaffe into a sharp-witted remark. Looking down, and forcing back a smile, he quips, "It will be the largest payroll, too."

The audience bursts into unanimous laughter, and he can't help but laugh now as well. It is the best line of the night, so typical of his easygoing personality, his ability to laugh at himself. It is his signature inimitable charm. The evening concludes with wild applause, another standing ovation, and as soon as the benediction is over, we hustle the president and Mrs. Kennedy through the crowd, out the lobby, and into the waiting cars.

Twenty-three minutes later we are back at Houston International Airport, where Colonel Jim Swindal has Air Force One's engines running so that we can depart as soon as all the passengers have boarded. There is still a throng of people here—whether it is a new crowd or the same people that were here on arrival, I have no idea. A row of Houston police officers is lined up on the tarmac, at President Kennedy's request, so he can personally thank a few of the hundreds who have done such a fine job during this brief visit. It is meaningful to the officers, and a wonderful gesture, but in the darkness it's far more difficult to scan the boisterous crowd, and we wish he would just move straight to the aircraft.

Finally seated on the plane, I look at my watch and note in my pocket-size daily diary the time we depart Houston: 10:15 P.M.

Sitting next to me, Kellerman looks as weary as I feel. The adrenaline has been pumping hard all day long, and we're not done yet. He pulls out the survey report for our arrival in Fort Worth.

"We've got leased cars again," he says. "Land at Carswell Air Force Base, then motorcade into downtown Fort Worth. Fortunately it's nearly midnight, so I can't imagine there will be big crowds."

Still, for the Secret Service, a motorcade with leased cars, at night, in an unfamiliar city is about as tense a situation as you can get.

10

Fort Worth

Carswell Air Force Base Arrival

There is a misty drizzle as Air Force One touches down at precisely 11:05 P.M., which means at least we won't have the tops down on the convertibles. But as Colonel Swindal brings the aircraft to the designated spot, I look out the window and I can hardly believe my eyes.

"Roy," I say to Kellerman, "take a look at that."

Standing in the pitch-black night, oblivious to the rain, is a crowd nearly as big as the one in Houston this afternoon.

"I'll be damned," he says, shaking his head in disbelief. "What do you think? Five, six thousand?"

"At least."

Once again Mrs. Kennedy heads down the ramp first, with the president a step behind. It's the standard routine now. There's no question that Mrs. Kennedy is a big reason for these massive crowds, and the president knows it. These are the photos that will be priceless for the campaign.

Governor and Mrs. Connally follow the Kennedys, and Kellerman and I are right behind. Once again, Vice President and Mrs. Johnson are there on the tarmac, wel-

coming President and Mrs. Kennedy to Fort Worth, another bouquet of flowers. Johnson reaches out to Mrs. Kennedy, smiling as big as can be, so proud of how his home state has come out for them. Kellerman and I race down the ramp, eager to get on the ground and get the motorcade under way. The cheering, shrieking crowd drowns out the loud jet engines and I go into a zone where I'm scanning every face as fast as I can while constantly keeping Mrs. Kennedy within an arm's length.

I'm stunned to see so many young children in the crowd. For God's sake, it's eleven o'clock on a cool, drizzly night. Seeing the president and first lady obviously means a great deal to the parents in order for them to want their children to witness this. I suppose because I'm around the president and Mrs. Kennedy all the time, and I've come to see them as normal human beings, this idolatry just seems crazy to me.

President Kennedy dives into the crowd, with Mrs. Kennedy in tow, reaching out, touching and making eye contact with as many as possible before Kellerman finally convinces him it's time to go.

I help Mrs. Kennedy get into the backseat with the president and Governor Con-

nally while Mrs. Connally slides in between driver Bill Greer and Kellerman. The doors close and I join the other agents in the follow-up car. This is our sixth motorcade of the day.

Fort Worth has gone all out to welcome these special guests. Buildings are decorated with Christmas lights and all the way into the city, men, women, and children stand at the side of the roadways in raincoats, holding umbrellas, waving. Unbelievable.

Fifteen minutes later we arrive at the Hotel Texas. The placard above the main entrance reads:

WELCOME TO FT WORTH
WHERE THE WEST BEGINS

But it's not the sign I notice, it's the crowd. Four thousand drenched people are pressed together, ready to burst beyond the flimsy barricades—the only thing standing between us and them. Fort Worth police officers are posted strategically, but they, and we, are vastly outnumbered.

The president gets out of the car and waves to the people calling out his name. I help Mrs. Kennedy out of the car and out of the corner of my eye I see the president walk briskly toward the delirious mob.

Dutifully, Mrs. Kennedy follows as women shriek at the sight of the handsome president and still others in the crowd call out, "Jackie! Jackie! We love you!"

The president stays with the crowd just a few short minutes—long enough that they can't say he snubbed them—and heads into the hotel. The lobby is jammed. Every inch of space is filled by a body, and still more are packed onto the open stairway. *This can't meet fire code,* I think to myself.

We push through the mass of humanity and get the Kennedys safely into the elevator and up to their room, Suite 850. Kellerman and I make sure the president and first lady are secure in their room and turn over the protective responsibility to the midnight–8:00 A.M. shift agents, who arrived earlier in the day and hopefully have had time to rest.

"Clint," Agent Kellerman says, "I've been advised that the president is adding another speech tomorrow morning, before the Chamber of Commerce breakfast. It's going to be outside, across the street in the parking lot, around eight thirty or so. As far as I know, Mrs. Kennedy isn't expected to be there, but you never know."

"Got it," I said. "I'll let you know if she tells me otherwise."

It is approaching midnight in Texas, but my mind and body are still on Washington, D.C., time, where it is nearly one o'clock in the morning.

Since leaving the White House at 10:50 A.M., we have traveled on one helicopter flight, three airline flights, driven in six motorcades, stopped at three speech sites, and encountered hundreds of thousands of people, if not a million, along the way. I realize that since breakfast at my home in Arlington, Virginia, this morning, other than a light lunch on Air Force One between Washington and San Antonio, I've had nothing to eat. I'm tired and hungry.

It has been a very long day.

DAY TWO

NOVEMBER 22, 1963

11

Fort Worth

Hotel Texas

Sound asleep in my room at the Hotel Texas, immediately next door to President and Mrs. Kennedy's suite on the eighth floor, I am jolted awake by the ringing of the telephone at six o'clock sharp. It's the White House switchboard with the wake-up call I requested last night. Prompt and reliable as usual. Other than being famished, I feel refreshed and ready for the day.

I order room service—poached eggs, home fries, bacon, toast, orange juice, milk, and coffee. If yesterday was any indication of how today will go, it's hard to say when I will have the opportunity to eat next.

I hear voices outside and walk over to the window. It is raining lightly, and although it's still dark outside, hundreds of people are gathering in the parking lot across the street, around a small stage. Everyone is dressed in rain gear and most have umbrellas. There is nowhere to sit, and the president isn't going to appear for at least another two hours.

Unbelievable.

While waiting for my breakfast to arrive, I shave, shower, and get dressed.

After devouring my breakfast, I go over the day's schedule again. It's a repeat of

yesterday—just different cities, different speech sites, and we end the day at Vice President Johnson's ranch. I've never been there before and I always find it interesting to see presidents and vice presidents on their home turf. That's where they feel most comfortable, and when they are out of the public eye you usually get a better picture of what they're really like.

Knowing Mrs. Kennedy, I am almost certain she will not join the president for the hastily scheduled outdoor speech—especially since it's raining. Yesterday was an unremitting baptism to campaigning, and while she held up remarkably well, it was obvious she was exhausted by the time we got to Fort Worth. Since she doesn't intend to go to the Chamber of Commerce breakfast, either, presumably she will take the opportunity to sleep in. Still, I need to check in with Kellerman and make sure nothing's happened overnight that I should know about.

I quickly pack up my things so my suitcase is ready to go before I leave my room. Someone from the White House baggage detail will pick up my bag, make sure it's on Air Force One and will be at the LBJ Ranch this evening when we arrive. At least I don't have to worry about my luggage.

I check the closet, the bathroom, and every drawer to make sure I haven't left anything. Double-check my pockets—commission book, wallet, sunglasses, the day's schedule. Revolver in my holster.

We have set up a security post outside the president's suite with a small table and a telephone that's connected to the White House switchboard, and when I emerge from my room, Roy Kellerman and Agent Emory Roberts, the supervisor of the 8:00–4:00 shift, are there waiting to escort President Kennedy outside to the parking lot speech site.

Shortly after 8:30 A.M., the president comes out of the suite with his two closest aides, Ken O'Donnell and Dave Powers.

"Good morning, gentlemen," the president says brightly, with a big smile on his face.

"Good morning, Mr. President," we reply in unison.

The overwhelming and enthusiastic reception the president received yesterday in three Texas cities was clearly invigorating, and today he appears to be well rested and eager for more of the same. The only difference today, if it continues to rain, may be that the tops will need to be on the cars. But, as we saw last night, even rain doesn't seem to deter his supporters.

Kellerman and Roberts get in the elevator with the president and his aides and they proceed down to the lobby. Once in the lobby, the other agents on the shift will move in, providing a loose wall of last-defense security around the president.

As I knock on the door to check on Mrs. Kennedy, I hear a roar of screams and thunderous applause coming from outside.

Inside the suite, George Thomas, President Kennedy's valet, is busy packing the president's things, while Mary Gallagher is helping Mrs. Kennedy. There is no hurry because Mrs. Kennedy isn't going to the Chamber of Commerce breakfast. Her next function will be the motorcade to Carswell Air Force Base and the flight aboard Air

Force One to Dallas. She peers out the window to watch what's going on down below, careful to keep her face hidden behind the curtain.

More applause, and then the president's voice ascends from the loudspeakers.

"There are no faint hearts in Fort Worth!" he declares.

A voice calls out amid the applause and laughter, "Where's Jackie?"

There's a brief pause. "Mrs. Kennedy is organizing herself. It takes her a little longer, but of course she looks better than we do when she does it." The crowd loves it.

In order to give Mrs. Kennedy as much privacy as possible, I return to the security post in the hallway outside the suite.

Soon Agent Paul Landis joins me.

"It's a madhouse down there," he says. "Five thousand people outside in the rain, and another twenty-five hundred in the Grand Ballroom. The president is in there now."

About five minutes later, the security phone rings.

"Agent Hill," I answer.

"Clint, it's Duncan." Bill Duncan is the senior advance agent for the Secret Service in Fort Worth. "I'm down here at the breakfast with the president. He wants you to bring Mrs. Kennedy down, *right now.*"

I pull out her schedule, and right next to the breakfast listing she has made a check mark in red pencil and written: *JBK won't attend.*

"But Mrs. Kennedy isn't intending on going to the breakfast."

"The president just told me to tell you to get her down here *now*. Everyone is waiting for her."

"Okay, Bill. We'll be right there."

I walk into the suite and call out, "Mrs. Kennedy? The president wants you down at the breakfast. Are you ready?"

"Come on in, Mr. Hill," she replies from the bedroom.

She's standing in front of the mirror, running a comb through her hair. She is dressed in her pink suit with the navy collar—one of her favorites—but I can tell she's not nearly ready. Clearly there's been a misunderstanding about her appearance at the breakfast.

"Good morning. I hope you slept well," she says cheerfully.

"We've got another long day ahead," I say. I don't want to rush her, but the president's message was clear. "Did you know that the president is waiting for you at the breakfast?"

She looks at me quizzically. "I wasn't planning on going to the breakfast."

"I know, Mrs. Kennedy, but I just got an urgent message that the president wants you down at the breakfast, *right now*."

She seems a bit surprised. "Okay, I just need to put on my hat."

Mary Gallagher helps her adjust her hat, pinning it on just so.

"Oh, and my gloves . . ."

I look at my watch. It's been seven minutes since Duncan called. Finally she's ready, and Paul Landis and I escort her down to the mezzanine level. I lead the way, walking briskly, with Mrs. Kennedy following and Landis behind her. The instructions are for us to proceed through the kitchen and enter the Grand Ballroom through a rear door. When we arrive at the door to the ballroom, I peek in to see what is happening. The room is filled to capacity with finely dressed women and men seated at rows and rows of long, narrow tables, and the master of ceremonies is drawling through the introductions of the dignitaries seated at the head table. There's Vice President and Mrs. Johnson, the Connallys, and a litany of local politicians and their wives. As soon as the MC's finished, I step into the doorway so he can see Mrs. Kennedy behind me.

His face lights up as if all his prayers have been answered and gleefully announces, "And now the event I know all of you have been waiting for!"

As Mrs. Kennedy walks into the room, all 2,500 people jump to their feet, applauding and cheering. The suddenness of the noise appears to startle Mrs. Kennedy, and it gives me goose bumps.

The room is so jam-packed, I can't believe the fire marshal would allow this many people in here. My goal is to get her as quickly to the dais as possible, following the narrow, clear path, without giving anyone the opportunity to grab her attention. Beneath the reverberating sounds of clapping hands, low voices divulge the impres-

sion she's already making. "Oh, isn't she lovely?" "My, she's even prettier in person!" "Look at that stunning suit!"

Everyone at the head table is standing as well, and as she walks across the raised stage, she looks out to the audience and smiles in appreciation of the rousing ovation. The president seems relieved that she's finally here—albeit twenty minutes late.

The people in the audience are buzzing—they don't care that she's late. They know what a rare opportunity this is to see the handsome president and his wife together, not whizzing by in a motorcade, but right here in the same room.

President Kennedy is introduced and he steps up to the podium.

"Two years ago, I introduced myself in Paris by saying that I was the man who had accompanied Mrs. Kennedy to Paris." Holding back a smile, he adds, "I am getting somewhat that same sensation as I travel around Texas."

The audience laughs. But he's not finished.

Glancing at Mrs. Kennedy, he adds, "Nobody wonders what Lyndon and I wear."

The room howls with laughter. It's so unexpected, so true, and so typical of President Kennedy's ability to connect with a crowd. It is a great moment, one that will be remembered forever by everyone here.

Another standing ovation at the end of the president's speech, followed by a presentation of gifts—a white felt western hat and a pair of cowboy boots for the president, and a pair of riding boots for Mrs. Kennedy. The crowd urges President Kennedy to pose in the hat and the news photographers are ready to snap a picture that will be on the front page of tomorrow morning's newspapers. But President Kennedy politely declines—he's not keen on wearing hats of any kind, and this isn't the image he wants plastered all over campaign posters next year.

Not wanting to leave the group with a bad impression, he returns to the microphone, hat in hand, and quips, "I'll put it on in the White House on Monday, and if you'll come up there, you'll get a chance to see it there."

Half the crowd laughs, while the others groan at his feeble attempt to appease them, but it doesn't matter. He's already won them over.

The hat is returned to the box and put in the able care of Agent Paul Landis, to be hand-carried aboard Air Force One, never to be worn by President John F. Kennedy.

There is just enough time to return to the suite for one short hour. Aides and visitors go in and out of Room 850, and before we know it, it's time to leave for Dallas. During this time, the drizzle has subsided, and through the scattered clouds the sun begins to appear. The tops have been taken off the convertibles, and as President and Mrs. Kennedy emerge from the dark lobby of the Hotel Texas, they look so happy.

The police have managed to keep the parking lot crowd well contained on the opposite side of the street, but as soon as the presidential party appears, the people clap and cheer, begging them to come and shake hands.

I brace myself, fully expecting he will cross the street, but surprisingly, he simply flashes a smile and tosses the group a hearty wave. Mrs. Kennedy gets into the back-seat of the white Lincoln convertible between the president and Governor Connally, while Mrs. Connally decides to ride in the vice president's car rather than squeezing in between Bill Greer and Roy Kellerman in the front seat again. There is some confusion and discussion about who is riding in the various vehicles, but it finally gets sorted out and the motorcade slowly begins to depart. Keeping my eye on the surrounding crowd of people, I jog alongside the presidential car for a ways before returning to the running board of the follow-up car. President and Mrs. Kennedy are talking and laughing with the governor, all of them so pleased with the way the day has begun.

The streets are lined with people all the way to Carswell Air Force Base. Entire schools have emptied so that the students can see the President of the United States drive by. Bands play at various points, creating a happy, festive atmosphere. It's a political dream—sunshine, large crowds, open-top cars, tremendous exposure—and a Secret Service nightmare. Oil and water.

Yet another large, enthusiastic crowd greets the motorcade at Carswell. They are mostly uniformed base personnel and their families, all of whom have come with the hopes that they might be lucky enough to touch President or Mrs. Kennedy. The Fort Worth Police Department has been immensely helpful, and President Kennedy takes the time to shake hands with as many of the officers as he can before boarding Air Force One.

Now it's on to Dallas.

12

Dallas

Love Field Arrival

The flight from Fort Worth to Dallas takes just fifteen minutes. It must be some kind of record for a presidential trip on Air Force One. In truth, it would have been a lot quicker to drive from the Hotel Texas to our destination in Dallas, the Trade Mart, rather than motorcading from downtown Fort Worth to Carswell, getting everybody on board Air Force One, flying to Love Field, and then motorcading through downtown Dallas all the way to the Trade Mart. There is just one reason for this flight. The political advisors want film footage and still photos of President and Mrs. Kennedy coming down the steps of Air Force One as they arrive in the Big "D," for use in the upcoming presidential campaign, and the exposure of a motorcade through the city, in the grand SS-100-X presidential limousine, with the top off. It seems like a waste of time and money to me, but then, in politics, image trumps efficiency. The repeated exposure may translate into votes, but it also provides far more opportunities for someone to harm the president and first lady.

During the flight, Kellerman shows me an advertisement that appeared in this morning's issue of the *Dallas Morning News*. The headline reads WELCOME MR. KENNEDY TO DALLAS . . . . but the text is anything but welcoming. It is a full-page,

WELCOME MR. KENNEDY

TO DALLAS...

...A CITY so disgraced by a recent Liberal smear attempt that its citizens have just elected two more Conservative Americans to public office.

...A CITY that is an economic "boom town," not because of Federal handouts, but through conservative economic and business practices.

...A CITY that will continue to grow and prosper despite efforts by you and your administration to penalize it for its non-conformity to "New Frontierism."

...A CITY that rejected your philosophy and policies in 1960 and will do so again in 1964—even more emphatically than before.

MR. KENNEDY, despite contentions on the part of your administration, the State Department, the Mayor of Dallas, the Dallas City Council, and members of your party, we free-thinking and America-thinking citizens of Dallas still have, through a Constitution largely ignored by you, the right to address our grievances, to question you, to disagree with you, and to criticize you.

In asserting this constitutional right, we wish to ask you publicly the following questions—indeed, questions of paramount importance and interest to all free peoples everywhere—which we trust you will answer...in public, without sophistry. These questions are:

WHY is Latin America turning either anti-American or Communistic, or both, despite increased U. S. foreign aid, State Department policy, and your own Ivy-Tower pronouncements?

WHY do you say we have built a "wall of freedom" around Cuba when there is no freedom in Cuba today? Because of your policy, thousands of Cubans have been imprisoned, are starving and being persecuted—with thousands already murdered and thousands more awaiting execution and, in addition, the entire population of almost 7,000,000 Cubans are living in slavery.

WHY have you approved the sale of wheat and corn to our enemies when you know the Communist soldiers "travel on their stomachs" just as ours do? Communist soldiers are daily wounding and/or killing American soldiers in South Viet Nam.

WHY did you host, salute and entertain Tito — Moscow's Trojan Horse — just a short time after our sworn enemy, Khrushchev, embraced the Yugoslav dictator as a great hero and leader of Communism?

WHY have you urged greater aid, comfort, recognition, and understanding for Yugoslavia, Poland, Hungary, and other Communist countries, while turning your back on the pleas of Hungarian, East German, Cuban and other anti-Communist freedom fighters?

WHY did Cambodia kick the U.S. out of its country after we poured nearly 400 Million Dollars of aid into its ultra-leftist government?

WHY has Gus Hall, head of the U.S. Communist Party praised almost every one of your policies and announced that the party will endorse and support your re-election in 1964?

WHY have you banned the showing at U.S. military bases of the film "Operation Abolition"—the movie by the House Committee on Un-American Activities exposing Communism in America?

WHY have you ordered or permitted your brother Bobby, the Attorney General, to go soft on Communists, fellow-travelers, and ultra-leftists in America, while permitting him to persecute loyal Americans who criticize you, your administration, and your leadership?

WHY are you in favor of the U.S. continuing to give economic aid to Argentina, in spite of that fact that Argentina has just seized almost 400 Million Dollars of American private property?

WHY has the Foreign Policy of the United States degenerated to the point that the C.I.A. is arranging coups and having staunch Anti-Communist Allies of the U.S. bloodily exterminated.

WHY have you scrapped the Monroe Doctrine in favor of the "Spirit of Moscow"?

MR. KENNEDY, as citizens of these United States of America, we DEMAND answers to these questions, and we want them NOW.

THE AMERICAN FACT-FINDING COMMITTEE

"An unaffiliated and non-partisan group of citizens who wish truth"

BERNARD WEISSMAN,
Chairman

P.O. Box 1792 — Dallas 21, Texas

(Political Advertisement paid for by Bernard Weissman)

harshly worded list of grievances, criticizing the president's policies, sponsored by an anti-Kennedy group called "The American Fact-Finding Committee." Another intimidating group has distributed thousands of flyers around Dallas with what appear to be mug shots of President Kennedy above the heading: WANTED FOR TREASON.

While we saw some picketing and minor protests in San Antonio, Houston, and Fort Worth, there was nothing as antagonistic as either of these issues. It is an indication that the people of Dallas might not be as friendly and receptive as those

WANTED

FOR

TREASON

THIS MAN is wanted for treasonous activities against the United States:

1. Betraying the Constitution (which he swore to uphold):
He is turning the sovereignty of the U. S. over to the communist controlled United Nations.
He is betraying our friends (Cuba, Katanga, Portugal) and befriending our enemies (Russia, Yugoslavia, Poland).
2. He has been WRONG on innumerable issues affecting the security of the U.S. (United Nations-Berlin wall-Missle removal-Cuba-Wheat deals-Test Ban Treaty,etc.)
3. He has been lax in enforcing Communist Registration laws.
4. He has given support and encouragement to the Communist inspired racial riots.
5. He has illegally invaded a sovereign State with federal troops.
6. He has constantly appointed Anti-Christians to Federal office: Upholds the Supreme Court in its Anti-Christian rulings.
Aliens and known Communists abound in Federal offices.
7. He has been caught in fantastic LIES to the American people (including personal ones like his previous marraige and divorce).

we've seen in the other Texas cities. Indeed, there was an incident a few weeks earlier, in Dallas, in which Adlai Stevenson, the ambassador to the United Nations, was heckled, harassed, and spat on. The Dallas chief of police, Jesse Curry, is concerned enough about citizens causing trouble that he actually made a special television address, appealing to the people of Dallas to be respectful during President Kennedy's brief visit.

Clearly the state of Texas is not uniformly behind a Kennedy-Johnson ticket, and that is precisely why they are here—to test the waters, and to use the Kennedy magnetism and charm to sway voters. Despite what appears to be hostile territory, the Secret Service has no specific threat cases in Texas. And that's what we worry about most—the ones who aren't on the radar.

The sun blazes against a blue sky, with just a few leftover clouds drifting by, as Colonel Jim Swindal brings Air Force One to a gentle landing at Love Field. I check my watch and mark down the time in my datebook: 11:40 A.M. Central Standard Time. It's my habit, and that of all the agents, to frequently check and record the time of pertinent events while on duty. Each shift leader types up a Daily Activity Report with the activity of their section and submits it to the Agent in Charge of the White House Detail. For the First Lady's Detail, it's just Paul Landis and me, which makes it a lot easier, but still, we are always concerned with accuracy.

As we taxi to our prearranged parking position, I can see a very large crowd gathered behind a fence line. Thousands of people with flags waving and a raised platform filled with press photographers and television cameramen.

Looks like another day of big crowds, which means a slow motorcade with frequent stops. As soon as the plane comes to a stop, the stair ramps are wheeled to the side of the plane. It's game time. My adrenaline flows and all my senses are at maximum alert.

The front door of the aircraft opens first. Supervising agent Emory Roberts and his agents on the 8:00–4:00 shift quickly descend the ramp to get in position on the ground. Seconds later the rear door opens, and as President and Mrs. Kennedy appear, the crowd goes wild. Whistles, shrieks, whoops, and hollers. It's especially tense for the agents for the next few moments because the president and Mrs. Kennedy are completely exposed as they descend the steps. Governor and Mrs. Connally deplane next, and finally, Kellerman and I race down the steps, using these brief seconds to get a feel for the crowd and scan the overall scene.

My eyes first go to those with the best vantage point—the people above the crowd. There's a television cameraman and a few others on top of a bus, scattered groups of people on the roof of a low building. On the ground, immediately at the bottom of the ramp, the local dignitaries stand in the formal receiving line, eager to greet President and Mrs. Kennedy, and hopefully get a photo for their own campaigns. Beyond them is a gathering of people who arrived on the press plane or the vice president's plane: stewardesses, pilots, crew members, and assorted political dignitaries, mixed in with dozens of reporters and photographers from the White House press corps. Beyond this interior circle is a mass of people behind the fence line—unscreened, unaccounted for, completely unknown to us.

Parked on the tarmac, close to the end of the receiving line, is the presidential limousine, SS-100-X, its flags already unfurled, and driver Bill Greer stepping in to

start the engine. Driver Sam Kinney is at the helm of Secret Service follow-up car SS-679-X, parked directly behind it. The rest of the motorcade—the vice president's car, press car, and staff buses—are all in place.

Win Lawson, the Secret Service advance agent who meticulously planned every detail for this leg of the trip, is waiting at the foot of the ramp. Agent Landis, who flew in on Air Force Two several minutes ahead of us, is already moving toward Mrs. Kennedy.

Once again the president and first lady are welcomed by Vice President and Mrs. Johnson—whom they just saw fifteen minutes ago in Fort Worth. Johnson introduces Dallas mayor Earle Cabell and his wife, who hands Mrs. Kennedy a large bouquet of red roses. Mrs. Kennedy smiles with delight, as if this is the first bouquet she's received. She knows the routine now, carefully juggling her purse and the flowers, leaving her right hand free for all the handshaking down the rest of the line. Political theater does not make much sense to those of us who see it up close from the inside. It just seems phony.

Plenty of young people are holding signs—WELCOME JACK AND JACKIE, WEL-COME TO DALLAS J.F.K., Kennedy and Johnson campaign posters—and there are lots of people with cameras, many still wearing raincoats. It's an exuberant crowd—much like all the ones we experienced yesterday.

We give the president and Mrs. Kennedy a bit of space as they go through the receiving line, and are ready to move in close as they head toward the waiting limousine. We are already five minutes behind schedule, and for an instant it appears that the president is going to adhere to the program and proceed directly to the car.

Suddenly he turns and strides directly toward the crowd. Mrs. Kennedy follows, her face plastered with a smile. She usually avoids these types of situations, so her continuing willingness to campaign like this really surprises me.

I make eye contact with Paul and we close in, keeping no more than an arm's length from Mrs. Kennedy, while Kellerman and Roberts cover the president the same way. It's mayhem. The crowd did not expect this bonus—my God, the opportunity to shake hands with Jack and Jackie!—and the people are going nuts.

"Over here, Mr. President! Over heeeere!" "Jackie! We love you!" "Welcome to Dallas!"

Press photographers are having a field day, crawling on top of any and every thing they can find to get a better angle. The president's agents and Paul and I move along the fence line as close to our protectees as possible. It is a very excited crowd and now we are surrounded with the mass on one side and the press behind us—like bees suddenly aroused, swirling in for the attack. It's a sea of hands—reaching, grasping—and bodies jostling. We are looking for that unusual movement, that out-of-place individual, someone who really looks different or whose actions are suspicious. Hidden behind our sunglasses, our eyes are constantly moving. We scan the ground for anything abnormal; look over the crowd to the buildings behind, up on the roofs. Back to the endless hands reaching and grabbing.

People often comment on the fact that Secret Service agents rarely smile, that we look so intense. That's because these situations always cause us deep concern. We

must be on the highest alert, all senses focused. We are not courting votes. We have one sole mission: protect these individuals at all cost. Nothing else matters.

After several minutes, the president gives one last handshake, turns to make sure Mrs. Kennedy is following him, and finally heads to the limousine. The photographers cluster as President and Mrs. Kennedy get into the rear seat through the right-side door. As Governor and Mrs. Connally fold down the jump seats and take their places in front of them, I jog around to the left side of the car to be as close as possible to Mrs. Kennedy. She places the red roses on the seat and looks up at me with a smile. The sun is so bright—it is almost directly overhead now—that she raises her hand to her brow to shield her eyes from the sun. Realizing her sunglasses would help, she finds them in her purse and puts them on.

I know how much she covets her privacy, and prefers to leave the politicking to her husband, but surprisingly, she really seems to be enjoying this.

13

Dallas Motorcade

As Bill Greer eases the car forward, I keep my hand on the door frame, jogging alongside on the left, while the president's agents take positions at other points around the car. When the president sees Mrs. Kennedy has put on her sunglasses, he says, "Jackie, take those off. The people have come to see you." That is the goal of this motorcade after all.

While the presidential vehicle is the flagship of this parade, the motorcade is rather long. It begins with a group of motorcycles, followed by a pilot car, more motorcycles, the lead car, the presidential limousine, and the Secret Service follow-up car. Four police motorcycles, two on each side, are positioned alongside the rear tires of the presidential limousine and the front tires of the Secret Service follow-up car, so as not to impede the movements of the follow-up car agents nor block the crowd's view of President and Mrs. Kennedy. Then comes the vice president's leased convertible, a leased Secret Service follow-up car, followed by thirteen more official cars, three buses, and some additional media cars. Finally, a police car and more motorcycles bring up the tail end.

The local authorities have provided 586 officers to help with securing the airport, the motorcade route, and the speech site. In Dallas the Secret Service has twenty White House Detail agents, four Vice Presidential Detail agents, and four agents from the Dallas Field Office—a total of twenty-eight. These agents are spread between securing Love Field, our arrival and departure point; the Trade Mart, the cavernous facility where 2,500 people are seated at white-clothed tables awaiting the president's arrival; and the motorcade through the city. Our resources are such that there are just eight agents working the presidential vehicle and follow-up car, plus two drivers.

Bill Greer drives the presidential limousine, with Assistant Special Agent in Charge Roy Kellerman in the front passenger seat. In the follow-up car, Sam Kinney drives, while supervising agent Emory Roberts sits in the front right seat. Agent Glenn Bennett from the Protective Research Section sits in the rear compartment with Agent George Hickey. Hickey is responsible for the AR-15 rifle that has been placed on the floor, out of sight, but within immediate reach. On the right side of the vehicle, manning the running boards, are agents Jack Ready in the forward position and Paul Landis in the rear position. I'm on the left running board, in the front, with Agent Tim McIntyre behind me. McIntyre was just assigned to the detail two weeks ago, so he's still learning the ropes.

We've also got two passengers in the follow-up car—presidential assistants Ken O'Donnell and Dave Powers. Eager to get film footage for the campaign, Powers has a movie camera with him, and being in the car immediately behind the president, he's got a better view of the adoring crowds than the press, who are farther back in the procession.

As the motorcade exits Love Field, the speed increases, the crowds disperse, and all of the agents assigned to the follow-up car drop back and jump onto the running boards of SS-679-X.

SS-679-X is a specially fabricated 1956 Cadillac four-door convertible, which the agents fondly refer to as "Halfback." The car is equipped with running boards on each side and specially designed handholds attached to the windshield frame. The running boards provide the agents a place to stand, and the higher elevation gives us a much better view to observe everything going on around us. Like the presidential limousine, SS-679-X also has small platforms built into the rear bumper and handholds on the trunk. A special compartment behind the driver's seat, accessible to agents in the rear seating area, stores larger firearms such as the Thompson submachine gun or the AR-15. Additionally, gas masks and gas grenades are available in this compartment. The vehicle has a built-in two-way radio system allowing com-

DALLAS MOTORCADE CONFIGURATION

LEAD CAR
Unmarked White Ford (hardtop)

Dallas Police Chief Jesse Curry	Secret Service Advance Agent Win Lawson
Sherriff Bill Decker	Secret Service Agent Forrest Sorrels

PRESIDENTIAL LIMOUSINE
1961 Convertible Lincoln Continental SS-100-X

Secret Service Driver Agent Bill Greer	Secret Service Agent Roy Kellerman
Mrs. Connally	Governor John Connally
Mrs. Kennedy	President John F. Kennedy

Dallas Police Motorcycle Officer

Dallas Police Motorcycle Officer

SECRET SERVICE FOLLOW-UP CAR
"Halfback" Convertible SS-679-X

Secret Service Agent Clint Hill

Secret Service Agent Tim McIntyre

Secret Service Agent Jack Ready

Secret Service Agent Paul Landis

Secret Service Driver Agent Sam Kinney	Secret Service Agent Emory Roberts
Presidential Aide Ken O'Donnell	Presidential Aide Dave Powers
 ———————— AR-15 Rifle ————————	
Secret Service Agent George Hickey	Secret Service Agent Glen Bennett

Dallas Police Motorcycle Officer

Dallas Police Motorcycle Officer

munications between it and the president's car, as well as to base stations and locations where agents have portable radio transmitters.

For most of us, this is our first time to Dallas. The route has been mapped out by the advance agent, Win Lawson, with the help of the Dallas Police Department, but the streets, the buildings, the geography, are completely unfamiliar to the rest of us. Each time we make a turn, we have no idea what's around the corner.

The motorcade proceeds down Mockingbird Lane to Lemmon Avenue to Turtle Creek Boulevard to Cedar Springs Road to Harwood. We move along around twenty-five miles an hour when the crowds are sparse, but as we approach the downtown area, the numbers of people increase, and we slow down to ten or fifteen miles an hour. After the complaints from the crowds in San Antonio about the motorcade moving too quickly, it seems like the president and his aides want to avoid the same criticism here.

Up ahead a group of schoolchildren are holding up a large hand-painted banner that says PLEASE, MR. PRESIDENT. STOP AND SHAKE OUR HANDS.

This is the kind of thing the president loves. Sure enough, he requests Bill Greer to stop, directly in front of the kids. They can't believe their luck, and in an instant, the entire group surges toward the car. Kellerman opens his door and stands at the ready—an intimidating figure—as the four of us on the follow-up car run forward and take strategic positions while President Kennedy stands up, reaching out of the car, laughing, delighted with the children.

As soon as he sits down, we get the crowd pushed back and we're on our way again. The crowds are really getting thick now—the sidewalks are packed ten and twenty deep with people waving, screaming, clapping. There is no sense of any hostility here—the people of Dallas have come out by the tens of thousands to greet their president. In some places, there are so many people the police officers can't keep them contained to the sidewalk and they're spilling into the street.

Bill Greer eases the car closer to the left side, to keep the president farther away from the encroaching crowd. This puts Mrs. Kennedy closer to the people—too close for my liking—and I immediately jump off the running board of the follow-up car, run to catch up with the moving presidential limousine, and jump onto the left rear step. I want to be in a position to intercede, if needed, to prevent anything from happening to Mrs. Kennedy. The crowds are so close that the motorcycle officer on this side of the car is forced to back off because there's no room to maneuver.

Prior to the trip to Texas, we were informed that President Kennedy had made a request that the agents stay off the back of the presidential limousine unless it was absolutely necessary. He doesn't want the agents hovering around him in these parade situations because it gives the appearance that we are a barrier between him and the people. He wants to appear as if he's one of the people—accessible, approachable. I know this, but it's also my responsibility to protect Mrs. Kennedy, and I'll do whatever it takes. If there's any complaint from the president later, I'll have no problem explaining my actions.

I hang on to the handhold, crouching on the step, until the crowds thin again. Off the step, onto the pavement, and back to the running board of the follow-up car. It's a challenging maneuver to jump from a moving vehicle onto the fixed surface of the road without going head over heels onto the street. The faster the vehicle speed, the more difficult it is. To get from Halfback to the presidential car while both are moving, you have to throw yourself forward with your feet and legs going at a similar speed as the vehicles. It takes timing, balance, and plenty of practice.

As we turn from Harwood onto Main Street, I'm crouched on the back of the car and can see that the crowds ahead are even larger than the ones we've passed, and growing as we proceed. Back and forth I go, between the two cars, mindful of both the president's wishes and my own comfort level with the situation to be able to do my job effectively.

There are people hanging out open windows, on balconies, and on rooftops. Now the people are ten deep, fifteen deep, twenty deep, pouring into the street on both sides, so that there is barely enough room for the cars to pass. People screaming, delirious with excitement, trying to break past the police to get to the president. This is the kind of situation that we, the agents, deplore. All we can do is remain vigilant, cognizant of everything going on ahead, behind, on both sides, and above as the passengers inside the car wave to the adoring crowd.

We've faced this same situation all over the world—Europe, South America,

Mexico, as well as in many other United States cities. God, in Mexico City there were *two million* people along the motorcade route, and so much confetti being tossed from open windows above that it looked like we were in a snowstorm. In Costa Rica, not even the military could control the surging crowds. In Billings, Montana, somebody passed their young child over the heads of the crowd so President Kennedy would touch him. The kid was damn lucky he didn't fall to the ground and get trampled. The world loves this president.

Ahead I see a bus filled with people, trapped on the parade route, taking up half of the already cramped street. Apparently the driver was allowed onto Main Street, intending to get ahead of the motorcade, but was stopped midway between intersections. The crowd has moved into the street, around the bus, and we have slowed to a crawl. This is a bad situation. I jump back on the rear step, directly behind Mrs. Kennedy, crouching, ready to pounce.

It's amazing, this crowd. Black people and white people standing shoulder to shoulder with their children in tow, all waving and cheering for the president. There's no hint of racial segregation or unrest here.

Moving along, still on Main Street, the number of people diminishes, allowing more space between us and them, so I jump off the rear step, bending my knees as my shoes hit the pavement, and in one swift movement grab on to the handhold and pull myself onto the running board of the follow-up car as it continues at a steady rate of speed.

We're coming up to an intersection, the end of Main Street. There's a building on my left that looks kind of like a castle, with turrets, arches, and a second-floor balcony, jammed with people. I'm about to jump back onto the presidential limousine. But as we get close to the end and begin turning right onto Houston Street, the crowds really drop off. I make the decision to stay where I am.

We make the right turn onto Houston Street. To my left is a large grassy area, a park of some sort, with a large concrete pergola, in front of which are some people,

but relatively few compared to what we've just been through. The president leans toward Mrs. Kennedy, a big grin on his face, and says something to her. I can't hear what's being said amid the noise of the motorcycles and the constant cheering from all sides, but she responds with a smile and a nod, clearly agreeing with him.

On the right side of the street are some high-rise buildings, with a few people on the sidewalk in front of them, but it appears we have reached the end of the downtown area. We've gone from twenty people deep on both sides to two deep at most. Finally, I allow myself to take a deep breath. This has been one hell of a motorcade.

Directly ahead of us is a reddish brick building, seven or eight floors high. Some windows are open, but nothing appears unusual. There have been high-rise buildings with open windows all along the route.

Up ahead, I see the lead car turning left, in front of the red brick building. The name of the building is etched into stone above the doorway:

TEXAS SCHOOLBOOK DEPOSITORY

As Bill Greer makes the left turn onto Elm Street, he slows way down and, following just five feet behind, Sam Kinney does the same. It's a sharp turn, less than ninety degrees, and maneuvering these oversized limousines, weighted down with full passenger loads, must be done with caution and care. Greer is cognizant of the president's chronic back pain, and turning too quickly on a sharp turn like this is something he always tries to avoid.

As soon as we turn onto Elm, the road slopes down as it approaches an overpass, which is directly in front of us, and we begin to slowly pick up speed. There are a few people on the overpass, but nothing appears unusual. The motorcycle officers are in place—two to my left and two on the right side of the vehicle. After the massive crowds we just passed on Main Street, it is noticeably calmer in this area. There's a grassy slope to the right with a couple of dozen onlookers—clapping and calling out to the president and Mrs. Kennedy. A sign indicates that the entrance to the Stemmons Freeway, which will take us to the Trade Mart luncheon site, is just a short distance ahead. This motorcade is nearly over.

14

The Shots

With my hand loosely on the handhold, my feet firmly planted on the running board, I scan the grassy area on the left side of Elm Street. Just a handful of people.

Suddenly I hear an explosive noise over my right shoulder, from the rear. Instinctively, I turn toward the noise, and my eyes cross the back of the presidential vehicle. I see President Kennedy throw his hands up to his throat and move violently to his left.

Oh God. Someone is shooting at the president.

I jump from the follow-up car and run toward the presidential car. My actions are automatic, reactive. The only thought going through my head is that I must get on the back of the president's car and form a protective shield behind President and Mrs. Kennedy. Nothing else matters.

The motorcycle engines are loud in my ears, and the car continues to move forward, away from me. I'm running as fast as I can, my eyes focused on the two people in the backseat of the car. I'm gaining ground, almost there, my arms reaching for the handhold, when another shot rings out.

The bullet hits its mark, piercing the back of President Kennedy's head, just above and behind his right ear. In the same instant, a vile eruption of blood, brain matter, and bone fragments spews out, showering over Mrs. Kennedy, across the trunk, and onto me.

I grab the handhold, get my right foot on the step, and suddenly the car lurches forward as Bill Greer steps on the gas. My foot slips off the step, back to the pavement, but somehow I manage to hang on to the handhold. Gripping with all my might as the rapidly accelerating car pulls me, my legs keep moving. If I lose my grip and fall to the ground, the presidential car will speed away, and the follow-up driver will have no choice but to run over me. Somehow—I honestly don't know how—I lunge forward, my foot finds the step, and I pull my body onto the car.

In the same moment, Mrs. Kennedy, covered with her husband's blood, her eyes filled with terror, is crawling out of her seat and onto the trunk. She doesn't see me; she doesn't even know I'm there. She's reaching for something on the trunk. *Oh God.* She's reaching for some material that's come out of the president's head.

The car is really beginning to speed up now, and if I don't get to her, she's going to be thrown off the car. I thrust myself onto the trunk, grab her arm, and push her back into the seat. When I do this, the president's body falls to the left, with his head in her lap. His eyes are fixed, and I can see inside the back of his head. It looks like someone has scooped out a portion of his brain and strewn fragments of skull, bits of brain tissue, and blood all over the car.

The president, without a doubt, has suffered a fatal wound.

"My God! They have shot his head off!" Mrs. Kennedy shrieks.

"Get us to a hospital!" I scream at the driver. "Get us to a hospital!"

As the car accelerates, I wedge myself on top of the rear seat, trying to get my body above and behind Mrs. Kennedy and the president, to shield them from what-ever shots might still be coming. Grabbing the top of the left door frame with my left hand, I wedge my left foot into the right side of the rear seat. Twisting around, I look back at the follow-up car and give my colleagues the thumbs-down sign.

In the car, Mrs. Kennedy is in shock. Staring at her husband, his head bleeding into her lap, she moans, "Jack, oh, Jack. What have they done?" And then, "I have his brains in my hands."

Quietly, she adds, "I love you, Jack."

Nothing else is said as we speed down Stemmons Freeway at about eighty miles an hour. I turn my head and my sunglasses blow off.

I can hardly believe my own eyes as I stare at the grisly scene inside the car. Mrs. Connally is crouched over the governor, and as she moves slightly, I can see his shirt is all bloody. For the first time, I realize he has also been shot.

We turn off the expressway, the car still going very fast. I shift my body weight to make sure I don't fall off, leaning into the turn, hands and arms on one side of the car, feet and legs on the other. It is a balancing act.

Time has stopped. It feels like an eternity before we arrive at the hospital. In reality, it has been just four minutes since the shots rang out in Dealey Plaza.

15

Parkland Hospital

The car slams to a stop in front of the oddly vacant emergency area at Parkland Memorial Hospital. I jump down from the car, looking around for someone to help. The president has just been shot, and yet there's no one there to meet us.

Agent Win Lawson jumps out of the lead car and runs into the emergency room. Seconds later he comes out wheeling a gurney, with a hospital attendant pushing a second gurney behind him.

The agents from the follow-up car, along with Dave Powers and Ken O'Donnell, rush to the president's car and, for the first time, see the grisly scene. Governor Connally is slumped over in the jump seat, impeding our ability to get the president out. The governor is still conscious and attempts to get up, but he collapses. We lift him onto one of the gurneys, Mrs. Connally gets out, and they race inside.

Mrs. Kennedy, still in shock and not uttering a word, is holding the president, his head in her lap.

"Mrs. Kennedy, please let us help the president," I say.

Staring blankly, she doesn't move.

On the other side of the car, Agent Landis urges, "Please let us help the president, Mrs. Kennedy."

Still no response. Precious seconds are passing.

"Please, Mrs. Kennedy," I plead. "Please let us get him into the hospital."

She looks up at me, her eyes hollow with shock. I've spent nearly every day with her for the past three years, and know her so well, I can read her emotions. It suddenly hits me. She won't let go because she does not want others to see the president in this condition. It is a gruesome scene, beyond the imagination. But worse, her husband's normally sparkling eyes are unblinking, his magnetic smile gone.

I pull off my suit coat and place it over his head and upper torso. She looks up at me and finally releases her husband. His feet are wedged under the jump seat, so Agent Lawson moves them, and together, Win Lawson, Roy Kellerman, Dave Powers, and I lift the lifeless body of our president onto the gurney.

Mrs. Kennedy holds on to the side of the gurney as we race into the emergency room.

Someone guides us past Trauma Room Two, where doctors are already working on Governor Connally, to Trauma Room One, and suddenly doctors and nurses appear from all directions. Medical professionals crowd around the president in the tiny trauma room, desperately trying to save his life.

Dallas police stand guard around the limousine. The decision is made to put the top on the car, to shield the bloody mess inside from gawkers or photographers eager to get a photo, and to preserve evidence.

The White House press and local reporters who were in the motorcade, too far back to see what actually happened, are frantically trying to figure out what's going on.

Agent Win Lawson, the advance agent, takes charge of securing the hospital. Nonessential employees are forced outside and agents take posts to make sure no unauthorized people get inside.

Back inside the hospital, Agent Kellerman asks me to contact the White House, while Agent Landis stays with Mrs. Kennedy.

The White House switchboard connects me to Jerry Behn, the Special Agent in Charge of the White House Detail.

"Jerry, it's Clint." I'm wondering how I'm going to explain the indescribable horror, when Kellerman grabs the phone from my hand. But before he can speak, a doctor calls out that the president is still breathing.

Kellerman hands the phone back to me and bolts into the trauma room.

On the other end of the line, Jerry Behn can sense the tension.

"Clint, what's happened?"

"Shots fired during the motorcade. Both the president and the governor have been hit," I begin. "The situation is critical, Jerry. Prepare for the worst."

The White House operator cuts in. "Mr. Hill," he says, "the attorney general wants to talk to you."

The attorney general, Robert F. Kennedy. The president's brother.

"Yes, Mr. Attorney General, this is Clint."

"What is going on down there?"

I explain that both the president and the governor have been shot and we are in the emergency room at Parkland Hospital.

"Well, how bad is it?" he asks.

A lump sticks in my throat. I don't have the courage to tell him his brother is dead.

I pull my emotions in tight and answer simply, "It's as bad as it can get."

Without another word, he hangs up. I keep the line open with Mr. Behn and suggest he notify the rest of the president's family members before they hear it from the press.

Inside Trauma Room One, the doctors work feverishly on the president. Vice President Johnson is now in a room down the hall, the door guarded by agents. Other agents are posted around the hospital, trying to maintain security. Everybody is doing the best they can, but nothing prepares you for seeing a man alive one second and his head exploding in front of you the next.

Ken O'Donnell, who was riding in the follow-up car and saw everything, is in sheer agony. He and the president are longtime close friends. Fighting tears, O'Donnell spots Agent Jack Ready, who he knows is a devout Catholic.

"Jack, can you get a priest to come to the emergency room? Immediately?"

"Of course," Jack says, his face tormented with pain. The reality of what has happened is sinking in.

I stay on the line with Jerry Behn, giving him a minute-by-minute account of what's happening. Two priests arrive and are escorted into the trauma room.

Moments later, Mr. Kellerman walks out and in a low voice says, "Clint, tell Jerry this is not official, and not for release, but the president is dead."

I knew it, of course, I saw the impact, but to say it out loud, to tell Mr. Behn, is difficult. President Kennedy chose Jerry Behn to be the Agent in Charge at the beginning of his administration, and the two of them had a close and respectful relationship. Normally, Behn would be on this trip, in Kellerman's place, but for the first time in three years he decided to take a few days off.

"Jerry," I say, "Roy says this is not to be released, but . . . but the president is dead." There is stunned silence on the other end of the line. I lay the receiver down on the desk and take a deep breath.

It feels like I'm in the middle of a nightmare. Truly, this is as bad as it gets. Down the hall, Agent Landis is with Mrs. Kennedy—I know he won't leave her side.

Ken O'Donnell approaches me, his eyes red, welling with tears.

"Clint, we need a casket for the president."

"Yes, sir."

Having never been to Dallas before, I have no idea who to call, so I ask one of the hospital administrative people if he can tell me the name of the best mortuary in the area. He takes me to a room near the trauma rooms in which there's a desk and a phone, and I call Oneal Funeral Home.

"I need a casket delivered to Parkland Hospital's emergency entrance," I say. "Right away. The best one you have." My voice cracks as I add, "It's for the president. The casket is for President Kennedy."

I return to the hallway, where Mrs. Kennedy is now sitting in a chair, outside the trauma room, as Agent Landis, Kenny O'Donnell, and Dave Powers try to provide comfort. She is still in shock, completely devastated. She was inches from her husband when his head exploded before her eyes. It is unfathomable.

When the casket arrives, I sign for it and help wheel it inside. The intention is to transport the president's body back to Washington, D.C., as soon as possible. The Texas authorities, however, tell us we cannot remove the president's body from the hospital until an autopsy is performed. State law requires that before the body of a homicide victim can be released, an autopsy must be performed in the jurisdiction in which the homicide occurs. The assassination of the President of the United States, at this time, is not a federal offense.

This is not acceptable to any of the presidential staff or to us in the Secret Service. How long will an autopsy take? The reply: depending on how difficult the procedure becomes—anywhere from three hours to a day or more.

This means Mrs. Kennedy would need to sit and wait for the autopsy to be completed. None of us are willing to agree to that. A heated discussion between O'Donnell, Kellerman, and the Texas authorities ensues. Our argument is that the president is the leader of all the people, and thus the autopsy should take place in the nation's capital. The Texas authorities insist the body cannot be moved. The tension rises, but I have no doubt what is going to happen. Texas law or not, we are taking the president's body back to Washington, on Air Force One, immediately.

Meanwhile, the president's body is put in the casket. When the local authorities realize they cannot physically stop us, a decision is reached that the autopsy can be performed in Washington as long as a medical professional is present with the body at all times, right up to the autopsy.

"We have the right man for the job," I volunteer. "Admiral George Burkley is the president's physician, and he's here. He can remain with the body."

For security reasons, it is decided that President Kennedy's death will not be publicly announced until Vice President Johnson leaves the hospital and is secure aboard Air Force One. Even though he has not been officially sworn in, constitutionally, Lyndon B. Johnson is now the President of the United States.

At 1:35 P.M. Johnson leaves Parkland, crouched secretly in the backseat of an unmarked police car driven by Dallas police chief Jesse Curry.

Finally, Mac Kilduff, the assistant White House press secretary, makes the formal announcement to the press. Within minutes, *CBS Evening News* anchor Walter Cronkite breaks into regular programming and, fighting back his own emotions, reads from the newswire: "From Dallas, Texas, the flash apparently official: President Kennedy died at one p.m. Central Standard Time, two o'clock Eastern Standard Time, some thirty-eight minutes ago."

Outside Parkland Hospital, the world has stopped. People listening to car ra-

dios pull over, unable to drive; women sob openly as men force back tears. Children struggle to understand why their parents, grandparents, and neighbors are crying. Whether they are young or old, black or white, the moment people hear the news is forever seared into their memories.

My emotions, as well as those of the other agents, must be suppressed because we cannot allow personal feelings to interfere with the job we have to do. We must act stoically. We do not know if this shooting of President Kennedy and Governor Connally is a singular act or if it is part of something much bigger. Some of the agents from the follow-up car have gone to protect Vice President Johnson, to bolster his protective detail. The agents that were at the Trade Mart have come to Parkland Hospital and are providing perimeter security. We must ensure the continuity of government at all costs. We must be more vigilant than ever. This is no time for us to mourn.

We all share a sense of loss. The President of the United States has been cut down on our watch. We have failed in our responsibility to protect him. That fact cuts deep into the heart and soul of every agent. But we must control our feelings. We must stay on task. We must maintain the proper decorum. The time for our grieving will have to come much later.

16

A New President

Paul Landis and I escort Mrs. Kennedy as the casket is wheeled outside to the waiting hearse.

Another car is positioned behind the hearse and, turning to Mrs. Kennedy, I say, "Mrs. Kennedy, we can follow the hearse in this car."

"No," she says. "I'm going to ride in the hearse with the president."

Admiral Burkley is already seated in the back, so I help Mrs. Kennedy get in and I climb in after her. There we are, Admiral Burkley, the casket containing the President of the United States, Mrs. Kennedy, and me.

At 2:04 P.M. we depart Parkland Hospital in the white hearse, its windows shrouded with curtains, and drive to Love Field in a silent, unannounced motorcade.

Air Force One stands on the tarmac, its engines running. The agents who accompanied President Kennedy to Dallas work together to remove the casket from the hearse. It is bronze, and very heavy. Fortunately, there are handles to help carry the weight. Now we must get it up to the rear door of the airplane.

Mrs. Kennedy stands at the bottom of the ramp, watching as we heave the casket step by step.

Even with all of us using all our strength, though, it is an extraordinary struggle to haul it up the narrow portable stairway. Every one of us is giving our all, honoring the president we love, in this heartrending moment we will never forget. Finally, we reach the top and the open door of the aircraft.

Carefully, respectfully, we begin to push the casket through the door. But it won't go. The casket won't go through the door. The doors of Air Force One are not designed to welcome a casket.

We realize the problem is the handles. With the handles attached, the bronze coffin is too wide to go through the door. We are used to working as a team, silently, with hand and eye signals. Not a word is said. Someone begins banging a handle

with his fist. The message is understood. Balancing the casket as best as we can, we use a free hand to force the handles up and down, pulling, banging, forward and back, using as much force as we can muster. They don't come off easily, but finally we manage to wrestle them off so we can get the casket through the door.

The Air Force One crew has removed seats in the rear compartment to create a space for the casket. The sight of the casket is devastating to the crew, who remained here at Love Field, and when Mrs. Kennedy comes aboard, her rose-colored suit encrusted with blood, it is almost more than anyone can bear.

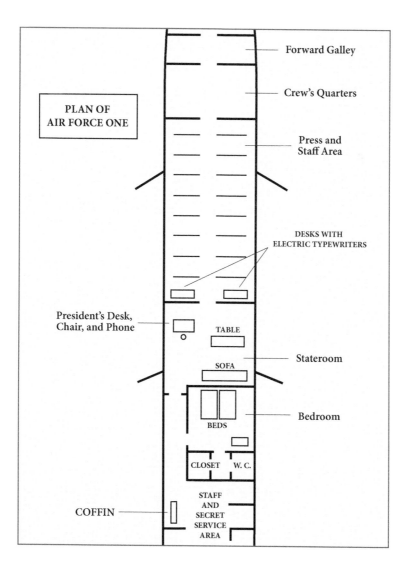

PLAN OF AIR FORCE ONE

Forward Galley

Crew's Quarters

Press and Staff Area

DESKS WITH ELECTRIC TYPEWRITERS

President's Desk, Chair, and Phone

TABLE

Stateroom

SOFA

Bedroom

BEDS

CLOSET   W. C.

COFFIN

STAFF AND SECRET SERVICE AREA

As the agents on the First Lady's Detail, Paul Landis and I stay with Mrs. Kennedy, but all the other agents are now concerned with Johnson. It strikes me that perhaps we should keep an agent with President Kennedy's body—out of respect for both President and Mrs. Kennedy, and in light of the questions that were raised at Parkland Hospital about taking the body back to Washington for the autopsy. This way, if there is ever any doubt about whether Dr. Burkley stayed with the body until the autopsy, or suspicions about tampering, there will be a Secret Service agent who also remained with the casket and can vouch for the integrity of the body.

Agent Dick Johnsen is selected for the post because he is an agent who was with President Kennedy from the beginning and is familiar to Mrs. Kennedy, O'Donnell, and Powers.

Mrs. Kennedy chooses to remain in the rear of the plane, near the casket, with Ken O'Donnell, Dave Powers, and Admiral Burkley. Once she is situated, I walk forward to find out the plans for departure. Vice President and Mrs. Johnson and some members of his staff, as well as members of Congress, are congregated in the presidential stateroom. I've been so preoccupied with making sure we could get out of Parkland Hospital and concerned about Mrs. Kennedy that I completely forgot that Vice President Johnson was waiting aboard Air Force One for Mrs. Kennedy and the president's body to arrive.

The area of the presidential suite is quite small, and now very crowded, as I make my way forward. It turns out we have another problem. The attorney general has advised that the vice president should be sworn in as president while we are still on the ground in Dallas. A federal judge is necessary to conduct the swearing-in ceremony and an attempt is being made to locate one. We won't leave Dallas until Lyndon B. Johnson is officially sworn in as the thirty-sixth President of the United States.

It's not long before Judge Sarah Hughes, who was appointed a federal judge by President Kennedy in 1961, and who lives nearby, arrives. White House photographer Cecil Stoughton is the only photographer aboard, and as he begins taking shots, more people swarm into the small space, all jockeying for a visible position in what will undoubtedly be the photo on every front page of every newspaper in the country tomorrow morning. I find it repulsive, but this is politics.

Mrs. Kennedy is still in the rear compartment, and before the swearing-in ceremony begins, I receive word that she wants to see me.

She stands as I approach her. As I look at her face, streaked with tears, her eyes so
hollow and lifeless, a wave of guilt and shame washes over me. She's just thirty-four
years old, and now a widow, with two young children.

How did I let this happen to her?

"Yes, Mrs. Kennedy, what do you need?"

She reaches out her hands, takes mine, and says, "What's going to happen to you
now, Mr. Hill?"

I clench my jaw and swallow hard.

"I'll be okay, Mrs. Kennedy. I'll be okay."

It is astonishing to me that she should be concerned about me at this time.
She has just witnessed her husband being assassinated and now must be present
for the swearing-in ceremony of his replacement; her clothes are stained with the
president's blood and brain matter; she is making no attempt to change or clean

up; and yet she is concerned about me, my future, and my well-being. She is a remarkable lady.

We are advised that the swearing-in is about to take place so I walk forward with Mrs. Kennedy to the presidential suite. Vice President Johnson asks Mrs. Kennedy to stand next to him as he takes the oath, and she obliges. I have no desire to be in the photograph, so I stand in the doorway, behind Agent Kellerman. Lyndon B. Johnson places his left hand on President Kennedy's Catholic prayer book and raises his right hand.

As he takes the oath of office, the reality of what has happened begins to sink in. Three hours earlier, we arrived in Dallas on Air Force One with a vibrant, charismatic president, whom I greatly admired and respected, and now we are returning to Washington with his body in a casket, his widow, and a new president.

It is a historic moment, but crushingly sad for all of us who witness it.

Mrs. Kennedy returns to her seat near the president's casket, and at 2:47 P.M. Central Standard Time, Air Force One is airborne from Love Field, Dallas, for Andrews Air Force Base, Maryland.

The flight to Andrews Air Force Base is surreal. You want to just break down and sob—and there are those who do—but certain things have to be done. The new president consults with members of his staff about organizing their administration. Mrs. Kennedy, Ken O'Donnell, and Dave Powers discuss what needs to be done upon arrival in Washington regarding the autopsy. Where will it be done? Walter Reed Army Hospital or Bethesda Naval Hospital? The radio operator is perhaps the busiest person aboard as General Ted Clifton, Admiral Burkley, and Roy Kellerman are sending and receiving messages dealing with the arrival and all the details that need to be in place before we land at Andrews. There is a great deal of confusion as people at one end of the aircraft are making decisions without consulting those at the other end. Admiral Burkley assumes the autopsy will take place at Walter Reed, while Mrs. Kennedy decides that it should be done at Bethesda, since President Kennedy was a Navy man. Plans are made, then changed. Mr. Kellerman seems to be the only one who really knows what is going to happen upon our arrival. He makes sure all the agents involved are fully briefed.

Prior to our touching down at Andrews, Dave Powers approaches Agent Kellerman.

"Roy," he says, "Mrs. Kennedy wanted me to tell you she would like the agents who worked for President Kennedy, along with those of us on his staff, to carry the casket off the aircraft."

Roy nods.

"And she wants Bill Greer to drive the vehicle being used to transport the president to Bethesda Naval Hospital," Powers says. He gulps, his red-rimmed eyes filling with tears, and adds, "She said how much Jack loved Mr. Greer, and all of you, and she knows how much you're suffering."

The only Secret Service personnel available on board to carry out her wishes are Kellerman, Greer, Landis, and myself. The other agents from the White House Detail traveling on Air Force One, those from the 4:00–midnight shift and the few agents who had been assigned to LBJ as vice president, are now covering President Johnson.

17

Return to Washington

Darkness has fallen on the nation's capital when Air Force One lands at Andrews Air Force Base. It is 5:58 Eastern Standard Time. As soon as the aircraft is parked and a stairway rolled to the front door, Attorney General Robert Kennedy races up the steps, through the passenger section and the presidential suite without acknowledging anyone, until he reaches Mrs. Kennedy and the casket containing his brother. No one was closer to President Kennedy than his brother Bobby, and it's a heart-wrenching scene as he and his sister-in-law hold each other, in shared grief, sobbing.

Outside, a hydraulic lift, normally used to raise and lower food or baggage to the passenger compartments, is raised at the rear door of the plane to facilitate the removal of the president's body. The door opens and those of us Mrs. Kennedy has requested lift the casket up and onto the waiting platform.

Holding hands, the attorney general and Mrs. Kennedy step onto the platform next to the casket. I join them, along with Mrs. Kennedy's secretaries, Pam Turnure and Mary Gallagher, and President Kennedy's devoted secretary, Evelyn Lincoln. Several thousand Air Force personnel are there to greet us, along with a large representation of senators and congressmen. Television and radio stations have sent crews to cover the arrival live. But unlike the arrivals we experienced in Texas, this one is marked by dead silence.

The lift is lowered to the ground as the world watches, still stunned that President John F. Kennedy is dead. Air Force personnel and body bearers from Fort Myer join the Secret Service agents in moving the heavy casket into the awaiting Navy ambulance.

"Mr. Hill," Mrs. Kennedy says, "Bobby and I are going to ride in the ambulance with the president."

"Yes, of course, Mrs. Kennedy," I reply. "Mr. Landis or I will be with you constantly."

The lift stops about three feet off the ground. Mrs. Kennedy jumps down, unconcerned with protocol or how she might appear, and approaches the ambulance with Robert Kennedy. Before I can reach her, she tries to open the rear door herself, but it's locked. I'm trying to get it unlocked for her, with no success, when the Navy driver realizes what we are trying to do and unlocks the door for us.

Mrs. Kennedy climbs into the back with the attorney general, Bill Greer takes his requested place in the driver's seat, while Admiral Burkley and Agents Kellerman and Landis cram themselves next to him on the front bench seat. I get into the first limou-

sine immediately behind the ambulance with Mrs. Kennedy's obstetrician, Dr. John Walsh, who has come here to be with her, and the three members of President Kennedy's "Irish Mafia"—O'Donnell, O'Brien, and Powers. At 6:10 P.M., our small motorcade departs Andrews Air Force Base, headed for Bethesda Naval Hospital. I can only imagine the emotion inside the ambulance or what, if anything, is said. All I know is that during the entire trip to Bethesda, I can barely control my own emotions as the three men in the backseat, three men who until this afternoon held more power than anyone other than the president, weep for the forty-five minute drive.

As soon as the motorcade is gone, the new president, Lyndon B. Johnson, emerges from Air Force One. He makes a brief statement to the nation, and then he and Mrs. Johnson, surrounded by the agents, board the Army helicopter and take off for the White House.

During the time Air Force One is en route to Washington, Dallas police apprehend twenty-four-year-old Lee Harvey Oswald. An employee at the Texas School Book Depository, he is arrested for allegedly shooting a police officer shortly after the assassination. Now in custody, he is being interrogated by Dallas law enforcement and Federal Bureau of Investigation agents.

If he is the assassin, the looming question is *why?*

At Bethesda Naval Hospital, Agents Kellerman and Greer accompany the body of President Kennedy into the autopsy room along with Admiral Burkley and General Godfrey McHugh. A special suite has been reserved on the seventeenth floor for Mrs. Kennedy and the attorney general to await the autopsy results. We set up a checkpoint to screen people because we know friends and family members will be arriving—President Kennedy's sister Jean Kennedy Smith; Mrs. Kennedy's mother and stepfather, Mr. and Mrs. Hugh Auchincloss; close friends Ben and Tony Bradlee; and Mrs. Kennedy's social secretary, Nancy Tuckerman.

Paul Landis and I wait outside to give them as much privacy as possible. We hear the soft sobs through the door and can do nothing but look at each other. There is nothing to say.

Meanwhile, President Lyndon B. Johnson has landed by helicopter on the south grounds of the White House, but he has no intention of staying the night. The mansion is still Mrs. Kennedy's and her children's home, and despite the fact that it would be the most secure place for him, he refuses to move in until the Kennedys have moved out. Instead he walks through the West Wing, across West Executive Avenue to his office in the Executive Office Building, where he makes phone calls and gets the security briefings vital to a new president.

At around 9:30, the Secret Service detail takes him to his private residence, the Elms, at 4040 Fifty-Second Street, fifteen minutes from the White House. As the vice president's house, the Elms had minimal security, but in the hours since the assassination, the Secret Service and the White House Communications Agency have installed new surveillance equipment, and a strong police presence is in place around the perimeter.

Lyndon B. Johnson finally has the job he has coveted and envisioned. But never did he imagine it would happen like this. With the power of the role, he has also inherited the sorrow of the nation. In his address at Andrews Air Force Base he stated humbly, "I will do my best. That is all I can do. I ask for your help. And God's."

At midnight, I realize November 22, 1963, has finally ended. It is a day that is seared into my mind and soul, a day I will relive a million times over.

What could I have done differently?

Could I have reacted faster?

Run faster?

For the rest of my life I will live with the overwhelming guilt that I was unable to get there in time.

DAY THREE

———

NOVEMBER 23, 1963

18

Autopsy at Bethesda Naval Hospital

The night drags on, interminably, as we wait for the autopsy to be completed. Agent Landis and I remain at the checkpoint, controlling access to the seventeenth-floor suite at Bethesda Naval Hospital, and this in itself is excruciating. We are the only ones who can identify the people who are allowed into the suite—we know all of Mrs. Kennedy's friends, and all the relatives. And they know us. It's so difficult to look them in the eyes as they arrive throughout the night. Stoically, we greet them, log their names and times of arrival. It is a great comfort to Mrs. Kennedy to have this time in private, beyond the glare of the press—to be able to cry and hug.

I check my watch constantly, comparing it to the clock on the wall. The hour hand seems not to move—it's like everything is in slow motion. At 2:45 A.M. the phone rings. It's Kellerman.

"Clint, we need you to come down to the autopsy room."

"Yes, sir. I'll be right down."

I hang up the phone and tell Paul where I'm going. He looks at me, his eyes pained with the knowledge of what I'm being asked to do. We have not discussed anything, he and I. Haven't talked about the horror we both witnessed, or the feelings of guilt and responsibility we both share.

Special Agents are not supposed to cry; there's no one to hug. We still have a job to do.

Paul simply nods. And I know he will take care of everything here.

Uniformed guards are posted along the corridor leading to the autopsy room and Roy Kellerman is standing outside the door, waiting for me. He's been through hell, too, and it shows on his face.

"Clint," he says, "I know this isn't going to be easy, but since you are closest to Mrs. Kennedy, we need you to see the body, now that the autopsy has been completed, in case she has any questions."

I clench my teeth; my jaw twitches. I know she will never ask me about the wounds. We will never discuss what happened today. But I understand this is something I must do.

There are more people in the autopsy room than I expected to see. Admiral Burkley, General McHugh, and Agent Greer are there, along with some other men in plain clothes, who are introduced as agents from the Federal Bureau of Investigation. A number of white-coated doctors are standing next to the table, which holds President Kennedy's body, covered with a white sheet. The lead doctor folds the sheet back, first exposing the president's head and then his torso. They've cleaned the blood from his face and his hair, and he looks so peaceful and silent, like he's just sleeping.

The doctor points to a wound in the throat and explains that this is where the emergency tracheotomy was done at Parkland Hospital, which covered up the area where a bullet had exited.

He rolls the president slightly onto his left side and points to a small wound just below the neckline, slightly to the right of the spinal column in the upper back. This, he says, is where the bullet entered, and then came out the front of the neck. The bullet that caused these wounds hit nothing but soft tissue.

Those wounds, I knew without a doubt, came from the first shot. It corroborates what I saw—the president suddenly grabbing his throat immediately after the first explosive noise.

The doctor points to a wound on the right rear of the head. This, he says, was the fatal wound. He lifts up a piece of the scalp, with skin and hair still attached, which reveals a hole in the skull, and an area in which a good portion of the brain matter is gone. I close my eyes for a moment, wincing, as the doctor keeps talking.

Difficult as it is, I try to focus on what he is saying. The fatal shot, he explains, entered the rear of the head and exited on the right, creating this flap of hair and skin. The impact of the bullet hitting the skull was so severe, it caused an eruption within that area of the brain, as the flap dislodged and was flung forward on the head.

Yes, that is exactly what happened. You don't have to tell me. I saw the president's head explode. His blood is still on my clothes.

"This was not a survivable wound," the doctor concludes.

I know. I saw his head fall into Mrs. Kennedy's lap. His eyes were fixed. I knew in that moment he was dead. I saw it happen. Heard it. Felt it. No one could have survived that.

It's all I can do to maintain my composure. Less than twenty-four hours ago, I saw the president happy, vibrant, and full of life. Now he lies here, silent, lifeless.

"Do you have any questions, Mr. Hill?"

Why isn't it me lying there under the sheet? Oh, God, why isn't it me?

"No, sir. Thank you."

He places the sheet back over President Kennedy's head. I leave the autopsy room with the images of President Kennedy's pallid, lifeless body and the wounds that killed him indelibly etched into my mind.

When I return to the seventeenth floor, some of the people who were so talkative earlier are now resting. Paul tells me the Irish Mafia has gone to Gawler's Funeral Home to buy a new casket, since the one from Oneal's was so beat-up when we tore off the handles—we can't bury the President of the United States in a damaged casket. George Thomas, the president's valet, is bringing several of the president's suits from the White House so the people from Gawler's can dress him.

At 3:30 A.M. Kellerman calls and tells us to get everyone ready to leave: the autopsy has been completed, and the president's body is now in the new casket.

Agent Landis and I stand with Mrs. Kennedy as the elegant new mahogany casket bearing the thirty-fifth president, now covered with the United States flag, is placed in the ambulance, and once again Mrs. Kennedy and the president's brother, Attorney General Robert Kennedy, get into the back with the casket. Kellerman sits in the right front seat and Bill Greer drives the president, one final time.

Immediately behind the ambulance, I ride in the front passenger seat of the Chrysler Imperial limousine we have always used for Mrs. Kennedy. In the rear of the limousine are Secretary of Defense Robert McNamara; the president's sister Jean Smith; the attorney general's wife, Ethel Kennedy; and Mrs. Kennedy's physician, Dr. John Walsh. Agent Landis rides in the car behind us with Dr. Burkley, Ken O'Donnell, Larry O'Brien, and Dave Powers.

It is a small motorcade, with no fanfare.

19

Return to the White House

It is still dark outside when we arrive at the White House at 4:24 A.M. on November 23. A large gathering of somber-faced spectators is lined up outside the gates, bundled in winter coats and hats. And as we enter the Northwest Gate, I see a unit of U.S. Marines, in full military dress, waiting at attention. The young men begin to march solemnly at port arms ahead of the ambulance, their chins held high, their boots hitting the driveway in perfect unison, providing their fallen commander in chief with a dignified and honorable welcome home. It is not something I expected to see, and my chest heaves with a sudden surge of emotion as I blink back the tears.

The procession stops at the North Portico entrance, and here a military honor guard is waiting to remove the flag-draped casket from the back of the ambulance. With tremendous dignity and strength, the staunch soldiers carry the casket in through the lobby and directly into the East Room as Mrs. Kennedy follows with the other members of the family behind her.

The East Room—where Pablo Casals played for President and Mrs. Kennedy in a historic performance, and where so many other happy occasions took place—has been transformed. A black catafalque, a replica of the one used for assassinated president Abraham Lincoln in 1865, stands in the center of the room, surrounded by wooden kneeling pews; black fabric covers the gold drapes like mourning clothes; and overhead, the giant crystal-and-gold-leaf chandeliers are draped with black crepe.

Mrs. Kennedy, surrounded by President Kennedy's family, his closest friends, and his staff, watches soberly as the honor guard places the casket onto the catafalque. She hasn't changed from her bloodstained pink suit—the same outfit she was wearing when I took her down to the breakfast in Fort Worth yesterday morning. It seems a lifetime ago.

The honor guard is posted around the casket to keep vigil. President Kennedy's body will remain here until tomorrow, when it will be transported to the U.S. Capitol, where it will lie in state for twenty-four hours. After praying with members of the family, Mrs. Kennedy finally decides to go upstairs to the living quarters to try to get some rest, for in a few hours she must do the unthinkable: at thirty-four years

old, she is the widow of the youngest President of the United States ever elected, and she must plan the state funeral for her husband.

I too am still in the same clothes I put on yesterday morning—minus my suit coat. It will be returned to me, days later, in a brown paper bag, and I will burn it along with the rest of my bloodstained garments. I am exhausted, my emotions shattered. I've been living on pure adrenaline. Before I go home, though, I go into my small office in the Map Room and scribble some notes about my recollections of the past twenty-four hours. As I sit at my desk, I recall the president walking out of the elevator the morning we left for Texas—was it just two days ago?—and telling me John will ride in the helicopter with us to Andrews. Thinking about John and Caroline, now without their father, is more than I can bear. Finally, at six o'clock in the morning, I leave the White House and drive the seven miles to my home in Arlington.

Two hours later, after a quick shave and shower and a light breakfast, I head back to the White House. It has begun to rain—a slow and steady drizzle from sorrowful gray clouds, as if the heavens are shedding tears of mourning, along with the rest of the world.

———————

Mrs. Kennedy has invited family members and close friends to attend a private Mass in the East Room at 10:00 A.M. The Kennedys are an extremely close family, and while they have lost their beloved Jack, they realize the world is mourning, too. This is the only time they will have together, out of the public eye, to pay their respects.

It is heartbreaking to see John and Caroline with the casket containing their father. John is still so young—he will turn three years old on Monday—that it's hard to tell how much he comprehends; but Caroline, who is nearly six and very astute, surely understands that her father is gone forever.

After the Mass, Mrs. Kennedy asks that the children's Secret Service agents take John and Caroline out, to keep them busy, so she can focus on the funeral arrangements. The three agents on the "Kiddie Detail" have become so attached to John and Caroline, as have Paul Landis and I, and for all of us, knowing these children will be growing up without their father is heartbreaking. The agents take the children on a long car ride, with a cousin, an aunt, and an uncle, ending up at their grandmother Auchincloss's home in Georgetown for lunch. In the afternoon, they'll go to Washington National Airport, where, from the VIP lounge, they can watch the airplanes taking off and landing.

After the children leave, Mrs. Kennedy calls for me. "Mr. Hill, I want to go to the president's office. Will you please get Mr. West?"

She wants to make note of the president's personal things so that she can take them with her. President Johnson has indicated that she can take her time moving out of the White House, but she knows he and his staff will be taking over the West Wing almost immediately.

I contact J. B. West, the chief usher of the White House, and ask him to meet us in the Oval Office.

The president and Mrs. Kennedy had decided to make a few changes to the décor of the Oval Office, and a new crimson oval carpet was installed while we were in Texas. Mrs. Kennedy wants to see it; the president never will. As we enter the office, on the main floor of the West Wing, yes, the carpet is in place, and it is beautiful. But much to our dismay, we are stunned to find that President Kennedy's things are already being packed and removed from the office.

As Mrs. Kennedy walks around the room, Mr. West takes notes of the things she points out. There is the glass-encased coconut shell from the president's PT-109 rescue, a collection of scrimshaw, and family photos.

"Remember when we found that desk, Mr. Hill? The president so loved that desk."

Shortly after President Kennedy's inauguration, Mrs. Kennedy made the restoration of the White House a priority. We spent countless hours searching through warehouses of furniture that had previously been used in the White House, and she found treasures in the most unlikely places. This desk, the HMS *Resolute* desk, which had been presented by Queen Victoria to President Rutherford B. Hayes in 1878, was being used in the White House broadcast room until she had it brought up to the Oval Office. President Kennedy did indeed love the desk. It has a unique trapdoor in the front, and he delighted in allowing Caroline and John to play hide-and-seek with it. Like the rest of the historical furniture in the White House, however, the desk will remain.

Tearfully, she walks over to the president's rocking chair and caresses it. This, of course, will go with her.

We don't stay long, and after one last look around, Mrs. Kennedy walks across the hall to the Cabinet Room and talks briefly with Mr. West about her plans for the funeral. From there, we walk along the colonnade, past the Rose Garden, the swimming pool, and the flower shop, in silence. We are both so very sad. No words are necessary.

Finally, she returns to the private quarters, and I go back to my office.

There is a pall over the White House as the staff and the Secret Service try to wrap our arms around this unforeseen tragedy. There are so many questions about the future, but for now, the priority is preparing for the state funeral.

20

Choosing a Burial Site

A couple of hours later, Mrs. Kennedy calls to tell me she needs to go to Arlington National Cemetery to pick out a burial site for the president. The president's family wants him buried in the family plot near Boston, but she understands his importance to history and that, as president, he represented all the people. She is determined, and taking charge.

It is around two o'clock in the afternoon when we arrive at Arlington—twenty-four hours since the president was pronounced dead. It's still raining lightly as Mrs. Kennedy walks around a portion of the cemetery, surrounded by the tombs of our nation's fallen heroes. Three of the president's siblings are with her—Attorney General Robert Kennedy, Pat Kennedy Lawford, and Jean Kennedy Smith—as well as Defense Secretary McNamara. It's not long before they find a large open area on a gentle slope that overlooks the Potomac River, the Memorial Bridge, the Lincoln Memorial, the Washington Monument, and the U.S. Capitol. It seems fitting, and finally the president's siblings agree that this is where President John Fitzgerald Kennedy should be laid to rest.

For the rest of the day, Mrs. Kennedy stays in the private quarters upstairs, planning what will be the largest state funeral in our nation's history.

Since returning to the White House at eight o'clock this morning, my entire focus has been on Mrs. Kennedy and her needs. There's been no time to think about anything else. When I go back to my office with Paul Landis, we learn that Lee Harvey

Oswald has been charged with the assassination of President Kennedy and is being interrogated. On the sixth floor of the Texas School Book Depository, where Oswald worked, detectives found a sniper's nest near the window; three spent cartridges on the floor below the window; and a gun believed to be the murder weapon—a 6.5mm rifle stashed in a corner near the freight elevator, also on the sixth floor. Oswald apparently fled the Texas School Book Depository immediately after the assassination, killed a police officer named J. D. Tippit, and was found hiding in a movie theater. The Dallas detectives are confident they've got the right man.

We sure hope the interrogators are getting some answers. What was his motive? If he wanted to turn the world upside down, he has succeeded.

President Kennedy inspired people to believe in hope and peace, to reach for the moon. During his short tenure, his message resonated around the globe, and now the world is in mourning. People by the thousands are flocking to American embassies to sign condolence books in London, Rome, Berlin, Paris, Warsaw, Moscow, Manila, and Tokyo. Stores have closed, sporting events are canceled, and all across America people are glued to their television sets, united in grief.

Finally, at midnight, once Mrs. Kennedy is secure and asleep upstairs, Paul Landis and I agree we should both go to our respective homes. Neither of us has slept in forty-two hours, and while we know sleep will not come easily, we need to at least try to get some rest.

Tomorrow will be another long day.

The White House is quiet and, as we walk through the halls toward the North Portico, we pass the East Room, where the honor guard stands at attention around the casket, as they will all night long, guarding the body of President Kennedy with dignity and pride.

DAY FOUR

NOVEMBER 24, 1963

21

Final Private Moments

Last night I was so desperately tired, and while my body craved sleep, my mind refused to allow it. I may have dozed on and off, but the events of the past two days kept replaying like a slow-motion horror movie in my head. My wife and sons were asleep when I arrived home—it was well after midnight—and this morning, as I forced down a quick breakfast, the conversation was sparse. They can't imagine what I experienced, and I can't bear to talk about it. I was eager to return to the White House, where I knew there would be an endless list of arrangements to make, and plenty of activity. Activity is the only thing that's going to keep me sane. Without it, there's only time to think.

Yesterday's rain has stopped, which is a blessing, for today is the day the president's body will be transported to the U.S. Capitol to lie in state.

It's eight o'clock when I arrive at the White House. My first call is to Provi, Mrs. Kennedy's personal assistant, to see how Mrs. Kennedy is doing.

Choking back tears, Provi tells me Mrs. Kennedy slept some, but it was a rough night. Fortunately, some members of the president's family stayed, and Mrs. Kennedy's sister, Lee Radziwill, arrived from Europe.

"That's good news," I say. Mrs. Kennedy and Lee have a very close relationship. Hopefully having her sister here will provide some comfort.

When Mrs. Kennedy emerges from the elevator, she is dressed in a black suit, with a knee-length skirt. Her eyes, which were so full of sparkle and light when we left the White House three days ago, are empty, lifeless. Her face is gaunt, and she looks so fragile, yet she still manages to say, "Good morning, Mr. Hill."

There is one last private Mass for the family in the East Room, after which she and the other family members return to the living quarters for a short period of privacy before they must face the public.

In the meantime, Jerry Behn, the Special Agent in Charge of the White House Detail, sends word that he wants to see me in his office, in the East Wing. President Kennedy appointed Behn to be head of the White House security detail shortly after the inauguration, and the two of them worked extremely well together. In the past three years, there was rarely a time that Behn didn't travel with President Kennedy. He was with him for weekends to Hyannis Port, Palm Beach, and Camp David, as well as every foreign trip. Behn takes his job so seriously that he has seldom taken a day off, and it was precisely because he knew he'd be gone from home much of next year with the campaign that he decided to skip the trip to Texas.

I haven't looked in a mirror, but the way Mr. Behn is looking at me, I can tell my emotions must not be very well hidden. I am a wreck, and he knows it. While he commends my actions in the midst of the gunfire, he can relate to the guilt I feel:

Nothing can change the fact that we, the Secret Service, failed to protect our president.

I've only been in his office a few minutes when a call comes in for me from General Godfrey McHugh.

"Clint, I'm in the mansion and we have a problem," McHugh says. There is no mistaking the urgency in his voice. "You better get over here to the East Room fast. Mrs. Kennedy wants to view the president."

"I'll be right there."

When I arrive at the East Room, Mrs. Kennedy and the attorney general are standing in the doorway, peering into the somber room. She has some envelopes in one hand and a large scrimshawed whale's tooth in the other. I recognize the scrimshaw as the one she gave to the president last Christmas. I helped her track down the artist, who was well-known for carving the presidential seal, and she told me how much the president loved it.

"What can I do for you, Mrs. Kennedy?"

"Bobby and I want to see the president."

"All right, Mrs. Kennedy. Let me make sure everything is okay."

General McHugh and I walk in and the general quietly requests the officer in charge of the honor guard to have his men leave the room.

"No," Mrs. Kennedy interjects. "Just have the men turn around; they may stay where they are. Just have them move a little."

The men of the honor guard solemnly, and in formation, turn an about face and take a few steps away from the casket. General McHugh folds the flag down, touching it with reverence, and together we raise the lid of the casket.

When I see President Kennedy lying there, so peaceful, it's all I can do to keep my emotions in check. Clenching my jaw, I swallow hard.

The general and I step back as Mrs. Kennedy and Bobby walk up to the open casket. Weeping with anguish, they stand looking at the man they loved so very much. Mrs. Kennedy turns to me and says, "Mr. Hill, will you get me a scissor?"

"Yes, of course, Mrs. Kennedy."

The usher's office is just across the hall, and I find a pair of scissors in the desk drawer. I have a feeling I know what she's going to do. I hand her the scissors, unable to look into her eyes, and take a few steps back from the casket to give her some privacy.

The scissors go *clip, clip*, and I assume she is cutting locks of her husband's hair—a part of him to keep with her. I turn and see the president's brother lower the lid of the casket, and then he and Mrs. Kennedy, both crying inconsolably, their faces tormented with agony, walk hand in hand out of the East Room.

As soon as they are gone, General McHugh and I check the casket to make sure it is securely closed. Out of habit, I look at my watch and take note of the time: 12:46 P.M. The casket will never be opened again.

As I solemnly walk past the Red, Green, and Blue Rooms back to my office, two staff members are talking in the corridor.

"That bastard deserves to die."

What?! After the emotional scene I've just witnessed, I'm about ready to throw a punch. How can anyone say such a thing, especially here, *in the White House*?

I wheel around, enraged. "What the hell did you say?!"

"Lee Harvey Oswald," the man says. "He's just been shot. The bastard who killed President Kennedy has just been shot and they think he's dead."

I'm relieved that my assumption was incorrect, that it wasn't President Kennedy about whom they were referring, but the news that his assassin is now dead is another crushing blow. Now we'll never know the answers. We'll never know why he did it. The mass pandemonium in the basement of the Dallas police station is being shown on live television, seen by the millions of Americans who have been glued to the nonstop television news coverage since yesterday. I haven't seen any television news reports, and there is no time for me to dwell on this now. The procession to the U.S. Capitol is about to begin.

President and Mrs. Johnson have arrived at the White House, surrounded by the agents on the 8:00 A.M.–4:00 P.M. shift—including some of the same agents who were in the motorcade with Paul Landis and me, two days ago, in Dallas. They are as shattered as we are, haven't had any time off, and are now responsible for guarding the new president.

A short while later, two buzzes indicates Mrs. Kennedy is moving, and momentarily, she comes out of the elevator with Bobby, Caroline, and John. As I escort them to the Blue Room, where President and Mrs. Johnson are waiting to greet them, I try desperately to avoid eye contact with the children—who are dressed in matching powder-blue coats, white bobby socks, and red shoes—for I know that if I look into their eyes, my emotions will get the best of me.

President and Mrs. Johnson greet Mrs. Kennedy and the children, and then together they walk to the East Room, where Kennedy family members and close friends have gathered.

There is a painful silence as the military body bearers remove the heavy casket from the catafalque and carry the slain president through the columned lobby toward the North Portico. It is a private scene, the last private moments they will have before facing the public and press outside.

Meanwhile, Americans across the country can hardly believe their eyes, as the live television news coverage switches back and forth between the simultaneous events of the ongoing chaos and confusion in Dallas and the grave scene outside the White House, as Mrs. Kennedy is about to appear in public for the first time since returning to Andrews Air Force Base the evening of the assassination.

Soldiers from each branch of the military slowly and deliberately carry the cas-

ket out the North Portico door of the White House as Mrs. Kennedy walks behind with Caroline clutching her left hand and John hanging on to her right. The three of them stand there on the steps of the White House watching military men move with precision, straightening out the American flag that covers the casket. They are at the forefront of those about to join the cortege. Standing at the bottom of the steps, off to the side with Jerry Behn, I feel absolutely helpless as they watch their husband and father being placed on a gun carriage. Caroline looks up at her mother for an explanation, while young John, who still does not fully understand what is happening, is much more infatuated with the men dressed in their colorful uniforms, lined up on the steps, than with the flag-draped coffin.

Meanwhile, at almost the exact same time, the news anchors on television report that the charged assassin, Lee Harvey Oswald, is being wheeled into Parkland Hospital on a gurney, and is placed in the trauma room at Parkland Hospital, just ten feet from where President Kennedy died two days ago.

Seven matching gray horses will lead the procession—three teams of two pulling the artillery caisson, with the commanding officer riding the lead horse positioned to the left of the front team. All six horses pulling the caisson are saddled, but only the three on the left carry riders, in the traditional military funeral procedure.

Behind the caisson is high-strung "Black Jack," a sixteen-year-old Morgan quarter horse mix that seems agitated and unable to stand still as the casket is strapped onto the caisson. This riderless horse, with boots reversed in the stirrups and a sword hanging from the rear of the saddle, will follow the presidential flag bearer just behind the gun carriage.

Mrs. Kennedy, Bobby, and the children will ride in what is now being used as the presidential limousine—a Cadillac—along with President Lyndon Johnson and the first lady, "Lady Bird" Johnson.

It is an awkward ride, for while President Johnson is the ranking leader in this procession, all eyes are on Mrs. Kennedy. It is the beginning of what will be a tear-jerking, two-day farewell to President John F. Kennedy.

22

President Kennedy Lies in State

The cortege gets under way, proceeding out the Northeast Gate of the White House. As we turn onto Pennsylvania Avenue toward the U.S. Capitol, people line the wide street, ten and fifteen deep on both sides, visibly showing their grief. The procession moves along slowly, deliberately, at the pace of the marching horses, and from my position in the front passenger seat of the Chrysler limousine I have a clear view of the tears flowing from anguished faces.

I have never been in a motorcade like this before. There are no cheers or shrieks, no political signs or waving banners. The only sound you can hear is the steady cadence of the muffled drums and the clip-clop, clip-clop of the horses' hooves. The nation has stopped to pay homage to its fallen leader, and around the world other nations are doing the same. There is a universal feeling of deep, profound loss.

When we reach the Capitol, the passengers in the presidential limousine get out of the car at the foot of the steps at the east entrance. Paul Landis and I stay close to Mrs. Kennedy while Bobby remains steadfastly by her side—he is her rock, and she his—and Caroline and John hold tight to their mother's hands. The children,

innocent-faced in their blue coats, stand out like two small angels against the sea of mourning grown-ups, all dressed in black.

The Air Force Band sounds four ruffles and flourishes and then plays "Hail to the Chief," slower and sadder than I've ever heard it before. Ordinarily played at 120 beats to the minute, Mrs. Kennedy requested the presidential anthem be played at *dirge adagio*, eighty-six beats a minute, and when she hears it, she begins to weep. Caroline can't stand to see her mother so sad; she looks up, and with sweet, caressing words, tries to console her. My face crushes with anguish, as I suppress the sobs that fill my heart.

It is military tradition to honor a fallen soldier with a twenty-one-gun salute, and the saluting battery from the Third Infantry, stationed several blocks away, awaits its cue. As soon as the band begins to play the Navy hymn "Eternal Father, Strong to Save," the first loud boom sounds, followed by twenty more, each spaced five seconds apart.

Against the backdrop of the melancholy music and the thundering cannons, the military body bearers remove the casket from the caisson and proceed toward the steps. An honor cordon of seventy Army, Navy, Marine Corps, Air Force, and Coast Guard members line the steps, while dozens of President Kennedy's aides and advisors, and a bevy of press, are gathered at the top landing.

The military pallbearers begin the long climb up the thirty-six steps, and while their faces are expressionless, I know what an extraordinarily strenuous task this is—it is much farther than the airline loading stairs up which the other agents and I

carried the president forty-eight hours ago. With the eyes of the world upon them, the young men ascend with supreme dignity.

With her head held high, Mrs. Kennedy takes her children's hands once again, and with Bobby alongside them, the four lonely figures follow the casket up the steps. A few paces behind, I try to remain a shadow, my hands down at my sides, my head down.

It is an interminable climb, but finally we reach the arched entryway that leads to the Rotunda. Senators, congressmen, and close friends of the family are already positioned inside, waiting and watching as the casket is placed on the catafalque in the center of the cavernous round room.

It has already been a long day, and John, who will turn three tomorrow, has been about as good as an active boy his age can be. He doesn't understand what's happening and when he begins to get rambunctious, Mrs. Kennedy gives me a look I know so well. I motion to the children's detail agents and two of them inconspicuously take John by the hand and lead him out of the Rotunda into a side room.

There are three eulogies—Chief Justice Earl Warren speaks on behalf of the U.S. Supreme Court, Speaker John McCormack from Massachusetts represents the U.S. House of Representatives, and Senate Majority Leader Mike Mansfield from Montana represents the U.S. Senate. Mansfield was a close friend of the president's, and his moving words are some of the most eloquent I've ever heard. But the most touching moment of all is yet to come.

President Johnson lays a wreath at the edge of the casket, and the room is silent. This is the end of the program—time to file out. But Mrs. Kennedy is not ready to leave. She leans over and whispers into Caroline's ear, and together they walk hand in hand up to the casket. Caroline looks up to her mother, following her lead. Mrs. Kennedy kneels, and her daughter kneels. The mother's black-gloved hand touches the American flag draped over the casket, and the little white-gloved hand does the same. Then, in a majestic moment, mother and daughter bring their lips to the flag, a final kiss to the man they loved so deeply, and who was senselessly taken from them far too soon.

Women heave audible cries, and tears stream down the stoic faces of senators, congressmen, generals, corporals, and Secret Service agents. Photographers hold their cameras through blurry eyes and capture this moment that brings the nation and the world together in heartrending sadness.

Finally, it is time to leave. The agents bring John to his mother, and as he looks up at the military men, covered in medals and awards for valor, he must wonder what could possibly have made such brave men cry.

Blinking back tears, the other agents and I accompany Mrs. Kennedy and the children back down the east steps of the Capitol. From this vantage point, high above Washington, I am stunned by the sea of humanity that awaits below. Thousands upon thousands of people stand in an orderly manner, queued eight and ten people deep behind a rope, waiting to enter the Rotunda. The president's body will lie in state until tomorrow morning, allowing the general public to pay their respects. We

gather into the cars and as we drive the reverse route back to the White House, we are met by a migration of people who are headed toward the Capitol.

The state funeral will be held tomorrow, and already we have received word that close to one hundred heads of state are flying in from all over the world to pay their respects. Mrs. Kennedy is well aware of the historical significance of this tragic event, and while there are certain protocols to follow for a state funeral, she wants it to be personal. One thing clear in her mind is that the procession will be a walking procession. Her intent is to walk behind the horse-drawn caisson carrying the casket from the U.S. Capitol to St. Matthew's Cathedral for the funeral Mass, and then across Memorial Bridge all the way to Arlington National Cemetery for the burial. It is insane.

Jerry Behn is deeply concerned about the security surrounding the funeral, and especially the fact that Mrs. Kennedy is insisting on walking.

"Clint," he says, "you're the only one who can talk her out of this. You must explain to her how dangerous this will be. If she walks, all the heads of state will walk, too. It's a security nightmare. Charles de Gaulle has had four assassination attempts on his life, and he's going to be right there in the middle of things. You've got to convince her this is a bad idea. We'll be sitting ducks."

I understand Behn's concern, but I also know Mrs. Kennedy, and once she puts her mind to something, it is next to impossible to talk her out of it.

I arrange to meet Mrs. Kennedy upstairs in the Treaty Room. She is alone, and invites me to sit down. She listens politely as I explain the concerns we have. Because President Kennedy was so beloved, we are expecting hundreds of thousands of people to line the routes between the Capitol, the White House, St. Matthew's, and Arlington Cemetery, and while we are using every available law enforcement resource available, we will still be undermanned. The fact is, our president was just killed in broad daylight three days ago, and now we will have a hundred more heads of state all gathered in one place. If anyone wanted to create chaos, there would be no better event.

"Please, Mrs. Kennedy, won't you reconsider your intention of walking with the procession?"

She thinks about it for a while and then offers a compromise. Out of consideration for our concerns, she won't walk the entire way—just from the White House to St. Matthew's. It's a little over a mile.

I relay the information to Mr. Behn, and while it's not what he was hoping for, at least it is not for the entire route. We will have one and a quarter miles of sheer exposure.

A few hours later, Mrs. Kennedy calls me.

"Oh, Mr. Hill . . . ," she begins. I know whenever I hear the words "Oh, Mr. Hill," I am about to get a request to do something outside the parameters of my job description.

For the past three years, I've almost always willingly obliged.

"Yes, Mrs. Kennedy?"

"Oh, Mr. Hill . . . Stash has just arrived from Europe and he really wants to pay his respects to the president. Do you think you can arrange it?"

Stash—Prince Stanislaus Radziwill—is Mrs. Kennedy's sister Lee's husband, and I've come to know him well. He is a fantastic guy and we've shared a lot of good times.

"I'll do what I can, Mrs. Kennedy. What exactly does he want to do?"

"He wants to go to the Capitol and I've heard you can't get in for hours. Can you help him?"

The emotions I'm trying so hard to bury come surging back as I think about Stash visiting the casket. He and the president were close friends and I know he must be devastated.

"Of course I can, Mrs. Kennedy. Tell him to meet me in the Diplomatic Reception Room and I'll take him to the Capitol."

I arrange for a White House car and driver to meet us at the South Portico. I open the back door and allow Stash to slide in, and then, automatically, I move to take the front passenger seat. I am a government employee, not a close personal friend.

"Clint," Stash says. "Come on and sit in back with me."

As we proceed block by block down Pennsylvania Avenue, we are both stunned by the crowds waiting to get into the Rotunda. A line—a mass, really—stretches around the Capitol, winding through Washington's streets for forty blocks. I've never seen anything like it.

I escort Stash to the front of the line and show my credentials to the officers stationed at the door. The scene inside the Rotunda leaves me breathless. In two separate lines, people file past the flag-draped casket, two by two, moving continuously, but as slowly as possible, to savor their precious moments with the dead president. There is silence but for the sobbing and sniffles, and the ceaseless whisper of feet shuffling across the Rotunda's stone floor.

I identify myself to the officer in charge of the honor guard and explain that Prince Radziwill is President Kennedy's brother-in-law and would like to pay his respects. Without question, the officer opens the velvet rope barrier so that Stash can approach the casket. As the anonymous mourners continue their orderly march

around him, Stash kneels next to the casket, his head in his praying hands, clutching a rosary, and convulses with sobs.

When I bid him good night later back at the White House, Stash looks at me, his eyes still pooled with tears, and says, "Thank you, Clint. I'll never forget what you did for me."

It is yet one more heart-ripping moment that will stay with me for the rest of my life.

Sunday, November 24, has been another day of unimaginable events. The press were piled up inside the Dallas County Jail awaiting the transfer of Lee Harvey Oswald this morning. When Oswald emerged, handcuffed to the imposing Dallas police detective Jim Leavelle, a man thrust himself through the crowd and shot Oswald point-blank. The shooter, Jack Ruby, is well known by local police, and he was imme-

diately taken into custody and charged with first-degree murder. Detective Leavelle accompanied Oswald in the ambulance and was with him the moment he took his last breath. After the bullet pierced him, Oswald never uttered a word.

So certain were the Dallas detectives that Lee Harvey Oswald was the lone assassin of President Kennedy that, within hours after Oswald's death, they formally closed the case.

It is just before midnight when I leave the White House, on November 24. I look down Pennsylvania Avenue at the lighted dome of the Capitol, where the American flag flutters sadly at half-mast, watching over the endless parade of mourners who, in extraordinary devotion and despair, are compelled to wait for hours in the cold blackness of night for the chance to say good-bye to their beloved president.

DAY FIVE

———

NOVEMBER 25, 1963

23

Procession to the White House

President Johnson has declared Monday, November 25, a national day of mourning. It is also John F. Kennedy Jr.'s third birthday. It is going to be an emotional day, compounded by unprecedented security challenges.

The president's body will be moved from the Capitol to St. Matthew's Cathedral, and then on to Arlington National Cemetery for the interment. The entire leadership of the United States will be present, along with leaders from almost every country in the world, and they will be outdoors marching through the streets of Washington, D.C., exposed like never before. It is truly a security nightmare, all conceived by the person whom I am responsible to protect—Mrs. Jacqueline Kennedy. The only thing I can do is to remain vigilant, focused on the job at hand, and pray that everyone else does the same.

When I arrive at the White House around eight o'clock, Paul Landis and I meet in my office to discuss the day's schedule. My first call, once again, is to Provi, to see how Mrs. Kennedy fared through the night.

"This place is madhouse," she says in her endearing, thick Spanish accent. "Too many people!"

She is frazzled with all the houseguests upstairs. All the president's siblings and their families are here now, as well as his mother, Rose. The one person missing is the president's father, Ambassador Joseph P. Kennedy. Confined to a wheelchair since his stroke two years ago, it would be impossible for him to come from Hyannis Port. But never before have there been this many friends and relatives staying overnight since the Kennedys have lived in the White House, and I'm sure it is pure bedlam upstairs. Provi tells me Mrs. Kennedy is concerned that John's birthday will get lost in all the other activity.

"We will make sure that John's birthday is recognized," I promise. "And it would help everyone if you can make sure Mrs. Kennedy is on time this morning. We are scheduled to leave at nine forty-five."

The military has a set procedure and plan for state funerals, and while Mrs. Kennedy has made a number of requests that alter some of the established traditions, the strictly timed schedule involves hundreds if not thousands of participants from all the military services and various branches of government. My experience with the Kennedys has been that they don't always pay attention to timetables, so I am somewhat concerned about staying on schedule. If we get a late start, it will have a domino effect on the entire day's agenda.

My anxiety is largely due to the fact that on this day, in which the focus of the entire world will be on Mrs. Kennedy and her two children, there are just five of us responsible for their protection. Bob Foster, Lynn Meredith, and Tom Wells will be with John and Caroline, while Paul Landis and I are responsible for Mrs. Kennedy. The rest of the White House Detail agents are assigned to President Johnson and his family. It has always been Mrs. Kennedy's desire to keep her children out of the public eye, and she has been successful in doing so, making the job of protection far easier for us. Today, however, they will be exposed like never before. You just don't know what kind of warped individual might be looming among the masses, ready to wreak havoc, knowing the world is watching.

At 8:30 A.M. the doors to the Capitol Rotunda are closed to the public. In less than twenty-two hours, more than a quarter of a million people have filed past President Kennedy's casket, with thousands more waiting all night, unable to get in in time.

Just as the private quarters are a "madhouse," so too are the public rooms of the mansion. All morning long, the visiting dignitaries arrive in preparation for the walk from the White House to St. Matthew's. In less than three years in office, President

Kennedy had personally visited with so many foreign leaders, both on their turf and his own, and had made such a strong impact that, upon news of his death, travel arrangements were made immediately. The unlikely gathering of kings and queens, presidents and prime ministers, from every corner of the globe is herded into the East, Green, Blue, Red, and State Dining Rooms.

Our scheduled departure time has come and gone, but finally Mrs. Kennedy emerges from the elevator—no one will bemoan the grieving widow for being a few minutes late—joined by her two brothers-in-law, Attorney General Robert F. Kennedy and Senator Edward M. Kennedy. Even in such desolation, she is a vision of elegance and grace, in a tailored two-piece black suit and a black hat, affixed to which is a sheer veil that shrouds her face. She has decided to allow Caroline and John to miss the brief ceremony at the Capitol.

I've arranged for the Chrysler limousine to be waiting outside, and as soon as Mrs. Kennedy and the president's two brothers are situated in the back, I take my place in the front passenger seat next to the White House driver.

Police have blocked off the route to the Capitol so that there are no other vehicles on the road, but the streets are lined with thousands of people standing shoulder to shoulder many rows deep. They have come from near and far—buses filled with students and caravans of families in cars, some having driven through the night from as far away as Minnesota and Maine. It is an overwhelming public outpouring of grief, and as we drive the short distance to the Capitol, the widow and the two brothers are deeply moved.

At the base of the Capitol's east steps, squadrons of soldiers and marching bands from all branches of the military are organized and waiting. There is silence as Mrs. Kennedy, flanked by Bobby and Ted, walks up the sweeping steps of the Capitol, with Agent Landis and me closely behind.

The military honor guard has kept vigil over the president's body, changing guard every thirty minutes throughout the night, and they stand there now as Mrs. Kennedy and the president's brothers solemnly walk up to the casket and kneel. They pray for just a few seconds, and then retreat, and walk back down the stairs, with Landis and me conspicuously in their wake.

As we descend, the body bearers remove the casket from the catafalque and carry it out of the Rotunda to the top of the steps. The U.S. Coast Guard Band sounds ruffles and flourishes and plays "Hail to the Chief." President Kennedy is about to depart the U.S. Capitol for the last time. Then, to the hymn "O God of Loveliness," the body bearers descend the steps with the heavy casket with such decorum that it appears as if the coffin is filled with feathers.

Once again, the casket is strapped and secured to the gun carriage behind the team of gray horses, and as soon as the family members are back in the cars, the procession begins. This time it is not the muffled sound of drums but the musical strains of the U.S. Marine Corps band I hear as we begin the slow pace up Pennsylvania Avenue.

Mrs. Kennedy requests that the windows be rolled down so she can hear the music. As we inch along, back to the White House, to the sounds of the trumpets and trombones, we see ladies weep into white lace handkerchiefs, men wiping away tears, and sailors and soldiers raising their right hands taut to their furrowed brows as they salute their fallen commander.

24

Walking to St. Matthew's

The procession enters the Northeast Gate of the White House and when we arrive at the North Portico, the entourage of dignitaries and world leaders is assembled on the steps. It is an extraordinary gathering: France's president Charles de Gaulle, Ethiopia's emperor Haile Selassie, Belgium's king Baudouin, Ireland's president Eamon de Valera, Britain's duke of Edinburgh, Germany's president Heinrich Lübke, Berlin's mayor Willy Brandt, Norway's crown prince Harald, Greece's queen Frederika, President Diosdado Macapagal from the Philippines, Morocco's prince Abdallah, Israel's president Zalman Shazar and prime minister Golda Meir—the list goes on and on. As Mrs. Kennedy and the Kennedy brothers step out of the car, the chorus from the U.S. Naval Academy is singing "Londonderry Air."

The plan calls for Mrs. Kennedy and several male members of the family to lead the walking procession, with President and Mrs. Johnson and the mass of dignitaries behind them, followed by John, Caroline, and their nanny, Maud Shaw, riding in the Chrysler limousine. But as the procession is about to get under way, Mrs. Kennedy sees how far behind the children are and says, "Mr. Hill, I want the children's car immediately behind President and Mrs. Johnson."

With more than one hundred of the world's leaders and their security details squeezed in the narrow driveway between Mrs. Kennedy and the children's car, this is not a simple request. But it is not impossible. I relay the message to the children's agents and soon I see the shiny black Chrysler emerging through the mob, led by Agent Tom Wells, as if he is parting the sea.

Now we can get under way.

As the Naval Academy chorus sings "Eternal Father, Strong to Save," the walking procession begins to march out the Northwest Gate.

Mrs. Kennedy's personal touch can be seen throughout this historic day, and one that most people will never forget is the sight and sound of the Scottish Black Watch bagpipers who march ahead of the horse-drawn caisson. The participation of a foreign unit in a funeral for the President of the United States is unprecedented, but their participation was something Mrs. Kennedy was determined to have. Twelve days ago, on November 13, Mrs. Kennedy had arranged for the prestigious military

brigade of the Royal Highland Regiment to perform on the White House lawn. The Kennedy family—who so rarely were photographed in public together—viewed the magnificent show of sword dancers and bagpipers from the Truman Balcony. With Caroline's arm around him, and John at times on his lap, the president had so thoroughly enjoyed this unique performance that Mrs. Kennedy could not imagine the president's funeral without them.

A company of Marines marches in front, followed by the Black Watch pipers in their red tartan kilts and white spats, their bagpipes echoing a poignant wail that seems to be synchronized with the clip-clop of the horses that pull the caisson bearing the body of President Kennedy. It is the utmost in pageantry, orchestrated by the thirty-four-year-old widow.

But the most poignant sight of all is Mrs. Kennedy herself, who leads the walking parade, her swollen eyes shadowed by a black veil. The president's two brothers march on either side of her, two loyal soldiers whose faces reveal the depth of their grief. Next to this tragic threesome are two men unknown to the crowd, faces wrenched with pain and guilt—Paul Landis, next to Ted; and me, alongside Bobby. Behind us come other members of the family; President and Mrs. Johnson, with their daughters, Lynda and Luci; followed by the car carrying John and Caroline.

Finally come the leaders from around the world, flouting caution, despite the tangible threats to some among them, to march in unity behind the determined widow. It is a stunning tribute to President John Fitzgerald Kennedy.

The children's agents, along with Agent Muggsy O'Leary, walk alongside the car, scanning the crowd, trying to keep their own emotions in check. The windows of the car are down, and as Agent Bob Foster walks beside Caroline, his hand on the door frame, suddenly he feels her little white-gloved hand reach for his. Whether she's reaching to him for her own comfort, or trying to console him, he doesn't know. But in that moment, it's all he can do to suppress the emotions that threaten to overtake him.

Church bells toll with the dirge of the Black Watch bagpipes as Mrs. Kennedy, her head held high like a Thoroughbred's, leads the procession in its slow crawl to St. Matthew's, setting pace in time to the rhythm of the pipers.

This is the dawn of the television age, and camera crews are filming every step of

this international event, broadcasting live. The assassination shocked the world, and for people to be able to watch the funeral live in their own homes, all across America and via satellite around the globe, is not only extraordinary, it is healing.

For the Secret Service agents, the walk is unparalleled tension, compounded by anguish. Everywhere we look, there are people. They are packed along the sidewalks, standing high above on balconies, and on rafters of an unfinished high-rise. If someone wanted to open gunfire or drop a grenade, there is no way we can protect this assembly of world leaders. But on this remarkable day, thank God, there are no loud explosions, no sudden shots ringing out through the canyon of buildings; there are only the sights and sounds of unrelenting grief.

President Johnson has declared this a national day of mourning in the United States, and at twelve noon, five minutes of silence are observed to mark the start of the funeral. Streets in cities and towns are deserted. Schools, offices, stores, and fac-

tories are closed. What little traffic there is comes to a complete stop. Buses and cabs pull to the side of the road. Trains and airliners delay their departures. People stop and silently pray on the street. The television networks have ceased regular programming to run the funeral uninterrupted, without commercials, and with a remarkable 95 percent of Americans watching, the events of this day are emblazoned into the nation's shared memory.

25

The Salute

We finally reach the Cathedral of St. Matthew the Apostle, and all the invited guests file in as the casket is moved from the caisson onto a bier at the front of the center aisle. Mrs. Kennedy takes her place in a pew at the front, with John and Caroline on either side of her, and I sit immediately behind them.

The Requiem Mass is extremely emotional, and once again, at Mrs. Kennedy's direction, ultimately personal. Luigi Vena, a tenor from Boston, sings the prayerful "Ave Maria," just as he did at the Kennedys' wedding ten years ago, while the archbishop of Boston, Richard Cardinal Cushing, who officiated the marriage and performed the services for baby Patrick's funeral just three months ago, is in command of the Mass today.

It isn't long before young John becomes restless. He has been so good all morning, but this is more than he can stand. It is, after all, his birthday. Mrs. Kennedy motions to Agent Foster, who immediately takes John back up the aisle to an anteroom.

At one point during the service, Cardinal Cushing refers to President Kennedy as "Jack, dear Jack." That familiar term of endearment strikes a chord in Mrs. Kennedy and she begins to weep. I anticipated the need for handkerchiefs today, so I brought along several. Leaning forward, I gently place one in her hand. She thanks me silently, with her tear-filled eyes, but all I can see is the sheer pain that's etched across her face.

When it comes time for Communion, I'm not surprised when Mrs. Kennedy stands up and walks forward to participate. As I have done so many times before when she and the president attended Mass, I get up and walk behind her.

Meanwhile, Agent Foster is trying to keep John occupied and has him practicing his military salute. About a month ago, Mrs. Kennedy asked Foster and the other Kiddie Detail agents if they would teach John how to salute properly so that when he accompanied the president to Arlington National Cemetery on November 11, Armistice Day, he could salute his father. We all joked about it because poor John just couldn't get it right—he kept using his left hand. At Arlington that day, John did it just perfectly. Now, two weeks later, however, John has reverted to using his left hand again.

A Marine colonel standing in the doorway sees what's happening and walks in to help. In his dress uniform, decorated with colorful ribbons and medals, he has John's undivided attention.

"John," he says, "no, son, you've got it all wrong. That is not how you salute."

Then, standing tall, shoulders back, the colonel jerks his right hand in a rigid, steady motion up to his brow and says, "*This* is how you salute."

John imitates the colonel, this time using his right hand.

When the service is over, John rejoins his mother and Caroline, and together they follow the casket out of the cathedral, down the front steps.

At the bottom of the steps, Mrs. Kennedy stands stoically as the casket containing her husband's body is placed once again onto the gun carriage directly in front of us. As the casket is secured, the military renders a salute to their fallen commander.

Standing just to Mrs. Kennedy's right, next to Ted, I see Mrs. Kennedy lean down and whisper into John's ear. Then, in a moment that is branded on my heart, young John Fitzgerald Kennedy Jr., on his third birthday, thrusts his shoulders back, brings his right hand taut to his brow, and renders the perfect salute to his father.

My chest heaves as I fight the surge of emotions inside. Looking around, I see that I am not alone. Everyone watching, from the Joint Chiefs of Staff to the lowest private, is struggling to remain composed.

Three years ago, I was there when John was born, and today we are burying his father. The inimitable salute is captured on film and becomes yet another iconic photograph of this tragedy. For the rest of my life, seeing that image is the one that will always, always choke me up.

From here the procession will drive by motorcade to the cemetery. The cars are lined up, ready to go, when Mrs. Kennedy informs me she has changed her mind and she wants the children to return to the White House with Miss Shaw, rather than attend the burial at the cemetery. We have not planned for this and have no available vehicle, but I give the instructions to Agent Tom Wells and he comes up with a solution. He confiscates the car assigned to the Joint Chiefs of Staff and motions for Agent Foster to bring the children quickly to the car. They make their getaway, leaving the Joint Chiefs furious and left to squeeze into other cars.

Suddenly Mrs. Kennedy is all alone, staring at the casket.

"Come, Mrs. Kennedy," I say. "Let me help you into the car."

She gets into the backseat of the limousine, and two former presidents approach the car. President Harry Truman with his daughter, Margaret, and President Dwight D. Eisenhower with his wife, Mamie, speak to Mrs. Kennedy for a few moments, expressing their sympathies, as Bobby stands nearby.

To see these two great leaders, both decades older than President Kennedy, who know better than anyone the risks that go with the job of President of the United States and have witnessed the horrors of two world wars . . . to see them fighting tears is yet another heartbreaking reminder of this senseless tragedy, that President Kennedy, at the age of forty-six, was taken from us far too soon.

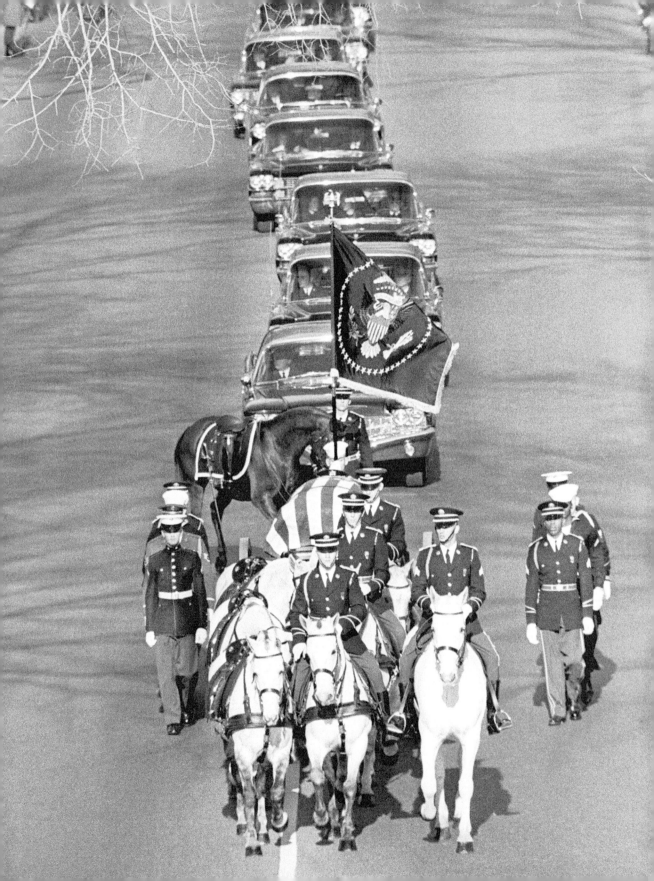

26

Burial at Arlington Cemetery

Finally the cortege moves out and we begin the final leg of the journey to Arlington National Cemetery. The streets remain lined with people, hundreds of thousands, quietly observing the passing of the commander in chief as we move ever so slowly toward the cemetery. Down Connecticut Avenue to Seventeenth Street, to Constitution Avenue to Henry Bacon Drive, past the Lincoln Memorial and onto Memorial Bridge. The cortege stretches for blocks, winding its way to the cemetery, a long black river of limousines filled with the dignitaries who walked to St. Matthew's.

The sidewalks on each side of Memorial Bridge are packed with people who stand in tearful silence as the somber procession crosses the Potomac River. As we move slowly across, I can see the area that Mrs. Kennedy selected as the burial site, directly ahead, just below the Curtis-Lee Mansion. I realize that each day from now on, when I drive to and from the White House, I will pass by the burial site, a constant reminder of that dreadful day in Dallas, a constant reminder of our failure to protect the president.

If only I had reacted quicker, run faster.

Greeting us on the green at the Memorial Gate entrance to Arlington National Cemetery is the Third Infantry Colonial Fife and Drum Corps, standing at rapt at-

tention. The Corps is a favorite of Mrs. Kennedy's and they have performed at arrival ceremonies for visiting heads of state on the south grounds of the White House.

We arrive near the burial site and everyone gets out of the limousines. The U.S. Air Force Bagpipe Band begins to wail the lamenting ballad "Mist Covered Mountain"—another special request by Mrs. Kennedy—and for the final time, the casket is removed from the caisson, then carried in a slow, rhythmic march to the grave site.

As Mrs. Kennedy walks with Bobby and Ted slowly up the grassy hillside, I hear the sound of jet aircraft approaching. Fifty jet fighters, representing the fifty states—thirty from the Air Force and twenty from the Navy—screech overhead in what seems to be an endless stream of three jet V formations. Then the final group roars across the sky in the missing-man formation, one jet short in tribute to their fallen

leader. Before the sound of the jets has passed, I hear a very high-pitched whine and immediately recognize the familiar sound of Air Force One, USAF aircraft 26000. In an instant, the whine turns to thunder as pilot Colonel Jim Swindal flies overhead, so astonishingly low it seems he will brush the tops of the trees. Then, with impeccable grace and control, he dips one wing—his final salute to the president he adored and served so well. It is a stunning, unforgettable sight and my heart cracks, knowing how much President Kennedy loved flying on that aircraft and how beloved he was to Colonel Swindal and the dedicated crew.

The graveside service begins with a silent drill ceremony presented by a special unit of cadets from Ireland called the Irish Guard. They had performed for President Kennedy when he visited Ireland and he had told Mrs. Kennedy how much he had enjoyed them. It is another personal touch, and it is remarkable that she has man-

aged to get them here. As soon as they finish, they march away, making space for the large number of dignitaries to move into position at the foot of the grave.

A row of seats has been set up alongside the grave for Mrs. Kennedy and the family members, and as they take their seats, Cardinal Cushing steps to the edge of the grave and begins the commitment.

"O God, through whose mercy the souls of the faithful find rest, be pleased to bless this grave and the body we bury herein, that of our beloved Jack Kennedy, the thirty-fifth president of the United States, that his soul may rejoice in Thee with all the saints, through Christ the Lord. Amen."

After leading the Lord's Prayer, the cardinal steps back.

Boom! The initial sound of the twenty-one-gun salute, fired by a cannon a short distance away, is startling to the civilians in the crowd, but the military ranks expect it, and in unison, they raise their right hands in salute. Immediately at the foot of the coffin, the incongruous sight of the towering Charles de Gaulle aside the diminutive Haile Selassie, both in full military dress, saluting their fallen comrade, is a moment that symbolizes the reach and breadth of President Kennedy during his short time in office.

Cardinal Cushing glides in to bless the casket, and now comes the part of the program I've been dreading. Three shots, or volleys, will be fired by a squad of riflemen. How will Mrs. Kennedy react? I saw her flinch at the low boom of the cannon, but the sound of a rifle, the same sound she heard just three days ago, in those seconds of horror, is going to be far worse. I stride toward her to warn her of what's coming, but before I can get there the cemetery superintendent, John Metzler, moves to her side and quietly alerts her.

Mrs. Kennedy shudders with each shot, but fortunately it's over quickly. A short distance away a lone bugler stands, bugle in hand, lips pursed, and he begins to play taps. It is a solemn moment and he alone has the stage before thousands in front of him and millions watching on television. He begins perfectly and then, on a high note, he falters. My heart sinks for him, but he recovers quickly and plays to the end with a memorable tribute to President Kennedy.

As the U.S. Marine Corps Band plays "Eternal Father Strong to Save," the eight-man military honor guard reach for the flag that's covered the coffin since leaving Bethesda Naval Hospital, and with white-gloved hands swiftly fold it into a rigid triangle so that only the white stars on the blue background are showing. They present the flag to Superintendent Metzler, who in turn places it in Mrs. Kennedy's hands.

It is a moment that seems so final. She clutches the flag to her heart, as if she holds the last remnant of her husband's life in her arms. Bobby walks toward her, and grasping her with his hands, offers her the consoling touch of the one person whose despair matches her own.

While she may not have known the procedure of the funeral until now, she realizes that what comes next is her most important stamp on this funeral, and on her husband's legacy. She moves the folded flag to hold it securely under her left arm, just as she did the bouquet of red roses she received upon arriving at Love Field, so that her right hand is free. A military officer presents her with a lighted torch, which she takes in her right hand, and at the head of her husband's grave, she ignites the Eternal Flame.

She hands the torch to Bobby, who touches it symbolically to the flame and then passes it to Ted.

This is Mrs. Kennedy's triumph. When thinking about an appropriate tribute to her husband, the vision of the eternal flame at the Arc de Triomphe in Paris came to her, and she knew that's what she wanted. She made the request, and it was passed to Superintendent Metzler less than twenty-four hours ago. Everyone said it could not be done. But she insisted. And here it is.

She thanks the commanding general, General Philip C. Wehle, for everything that's been done on behalf of President Kennedy. Bobby grabs her hand in his, and together they walk away.

27

Return to the White House

The day is not over. Mrs. Kennedy has planned a reception for all the heads of state who traveled so far to pay their respects. On arrival at the White House she immediately goes to the second-floor living quarters to freshen up and prepare to receive her guests.

First are a small group of dignitaries, personally selected by Mrs. Kennedy to be received on the second floor in the Yellow Oval Room. They include Emperor Haile Selassie, President Charles de Gaulle, President Eamon de Valera, and Prince Philip, the Duke of Edinburgh, representing the United Kingdom.

Downstairs, in the Red Room, the remaining dignitaries are assembled, and Mrs. Kennedy stands in a reception line to receive them. Tired as she is, she manages to retain her composure and thank each and every one of the dignitaries in attendance. Even as some of them weep before her, she somehow stands strong. I am so proud of her. I know, because I know her like no one else does, that she is not the delicate flower so many people perceive her to be. She has had every right to fall apart in these last few days, and yes, there were private moments when she did, but she has been a model of grace and dignity, a pillar of strength to the entire nation.

Finally, when the protocol is finished and Mrs. Kennedy is preparing to go to the second-floor residence, she motions to me.

"Yes, Mrs. Kennedy, what can I do for you?"

"I may want to go back to Arlington later," she whispers. "I'll call and let you know."

"Yes, of course, Mrs. Kennedy," I answer. "Oh, and Mrs. Kennedy . . ."

It has been such an emotionally draining day and her eyes are so empty that I hesitate to remind her.

"What is it, Mr. Hill?"

"I hate to bring it up, but I told Provi I'd remind you. Have you thought about doing anything for John's birthday?"

Her mouth breaks into the slightest of smiles. "Oh, Mr. Hill, you never forget anything, do you? In fact, that's what we're going to do now. Everyone's upstairs and

we're going to have a little celebration. Then we'll have a joint party for John and Caroline in a few days."

Mrs. Kennedy takes the elevator to the second-floor residence, where members of the Robert Kennedy, Lawford, Smith, Radziwill, and Auchincloss families have gathered in the family dining room. President Kennedy's dear friend Dave Powers leads the subdued festivities with Irish songs and silly poems. There are presents and cake, and the laughter of the children is a sliver of sunshine amid the blackness of the past four days.

Both Agent Landis and I are exhausted, but if Mrs. Kennedy has enough strength left to return to the grave site, we are going to make sure she can do it. I notify Superintendent Metzler of our impending visit, and then call Sergeant Irv Watkins, one of our loyal White House drivers, and advise him we will probably be needing him and the car later.

It is nearly midnight when the phone in my office rings.

"Yes, Mrs. Kennedy?"

"Mr. Hill, Bobby and I want to go to Arlington now. We want to see the flame."

We drive in silence through the now dark and empty streets of the nation's capital, past the Lincoln Memorial, and as we turn onto Memorial Bridge, flickering in front of us is the Eternal Flame. It is an emotional sight for all.

We enter the gates of the cemetery and Watkins parks near the grave site as Agent Landis, in the follow-up car, joins us. Landis and I follow Mrs. Kennedy and her brother-in-law up the slope to the grave. It is so dark, yet so peaceful. Mrs. Kennedy has brought a small bouquet of flowers from the White House to place on the grave, and she is somewhat surprised to find some wreaths of flowers, military caps, and mementos that have already been placed there. She sees them for what they are

meant to be—tributes to her husband. As Paul and I stand a few yards away, Bobby and Mrs. Kennedy kneel and pray together. They look across the Potomac to the spectacular view of the city.

It is a short visit, but it means so much to Mrs. Kennedy and Bobby to have this private time with their beloved Jack. We return to the White House, and as I say good night to Mrs. Kennedy, telling her I'll see her in the morning, she reminds me, with the slightest hint of a smile, that it already is morning.

"And thank you, Mr. Hill. Thank you."

I walk into the White House Diplomatic Reception Room and it hits me that just five days ago, I was standing here with President and Mrs. Kennedy and young John waiting for the helicopter to arrive to begin the trip to Texas. It started out with such hope, promise, and high expectations. Who could have predicted how the world would change in an instant. But that is exactly what happened.

On November 22, 1963, three shots were fired in Dallas, and the world stopped for four days. It was the end of the age of innocence.

For Clint Hill —
    Who did more than anyone to
make my life with the President happy —
and who guarded and protected him until
the very end — How can I thank you
                Jacqueline Kennedy

Epilogue

The motorcade in Dallas, Texas, began like countless others I had worked with President and Mrs. Kennedy. There were dense crowds and screams of adoration all along the route. Then, five minutes from our destination, the crowds dwindled, and out of nowhere, three shots rang out in Dealey Plaza. Time stopped. It was almost incomprehensible—the President of the United States was dead. In this new age of television, the news spread like nothing ever had before; Americans and people all over the world experienced this tragedy together. It felt like you'd lost a member of your own family.

When Lee Harvey Oswald was arrested, there was a wave of disbelief. How could one man, an insignificant loner who couldn't hold a job and had deep-seated emotional problems, be solely responsible for this heinous act? It just didn't seem fitting for the death of a president. Then, when millions watched Jack Ruby shoot Oswald point-blank on live television, another shock wave resonated around the world.

It felt as if America were coming apart at the seams.

Fifty years later, countless myths continue to be perpetuated and debated in films, documentaries, books, and blogs, in an endless quest for justification. The information presented by the majority of these people is theory, not fact. They were not witnesses to the assassination, have little or no knowledge of protective procedures, did not know the depth of the dedication of the Secret Service agents on this assignment, and cannot possibly comprehend what those of us in that motorcade experienced. The truth is simple.

On Friday, November 22, 1963, three shots were fired as President Kennedy's motorcade passed through Dealey Plaza in Dallas, Texas.

I was on the left running board, in the forward position, immediately behind the presidential limousine.

I heard the first shot and saw President Kennedy's violent reaction as it pierced him in the upper back and came out his throat. The wound would not have been fatal.

I knew immediately that something was wrong and I jumped off the follow-up car and ran toward the president's limousine.

While I was running, there was a second shot. I did not hear it. The motorcycle engines were loud in my ears, and all my senses were focused on getting to the back of that car to form a shield above President and Mrs. Kennedy to prevent any further damage.

But from all the evidence and testimony that came from valid witnesses, there is no doubt in my mind that there was a second shot at this time. This shot, the second shot, hit Governor Connally.

Mrs. Connally, who was sitting next to the governor and did hear the second shot, also had no doubt that this was the shot that hit her husband.

Then there was a third shot. This one I heard, and I saw its immediate effects.

In reaction to the first shot, President Kennedy's head was turned toward Mrs. Kennedy in such a way that when the third bullet pierced the back of his skull, it exited out the right side of his head.

This was the fatal shot.

All three shots came from the same location—the sixth floor of the Texas School Book Depository. One man fired all three shots, and his name was Lee Harvey Oswald.

The President of the United States was struck down in the prime of his life by a lone assassin. It was not a military coup or the work of a conspiracy. It was the act of one man, acting alone. Three shots. One gunman. All from the same location.

I am often asked why I was the only agent that reacted. The simple fact is that I was the only one who had a chance. If you look at the photograph that was taken by James Altgens on Elm Street, at almost exactly the moment the first shot hit President Kennedy, you can see this is true.

I had been scanning the area to my left, when I heard a sudden explosive sound over my right shoulder. It came from an elevated position, and instinctively I started to turn my head toward that sound. In so doing, my gaze passed across the back of the presidential limousine, and I saw the president grab at his throat. You can see the president's hand at his neck in the photo. Behind me, Agent Tim McIntyre also turned toward the noise, but because of his position, he didn't see the president's reaction.

On the right-side running boards of the follow-up car, both Agent Jack Ready, in the forward position, and Agent Paul Landis, in the rear position, had been scanning the crowds to the right of the vehicle, and at the sound of the first shot, their heads also turned automatically toward the explosive sound—away from the president. By the time these agents turned back toward the presidential limousine, I was already off and running. The next two shots came in rapid succession, and it was already too late for them to respond.

In the rear seat of the follow-up car, Agent George Hickey, who was manning the AR-15 rifle, also turned back toward the Texas School Book Depository, so much so that in this photo you see only the back of his head.

People ask, "What about Roy Kellerman, who was in the front right seat of the presidential limousine? Why didn't he jump in the back?" Again, the answer is simple. There was a permanently fixed wide metal bar that ran from the left side of the limousine to the right, just behind and above the front seat, onto which the various tops of the car were attached when in use. But even without the tops on, the position of this bar precluded whoever was in that front seat from having immediate access to the passengers in the back. Additionally, Governor and Mrs. Connally were in the jump seats, and Kellerman would have had to climb over them to get to the president. The car was designed for political purposes more than it was meant to be a protective vehicle.

I was the only one who had a chance.

There is another interesting thing to note in this particular photograph. Look at the motorcycle officer positioned immediately to the right of the presidential limousine, on the left-hand side of the photo. He too is looking back toward the origination of that first shot. And look at some of the people in the crowd on the left-hand side of the photo. Many of them are looking back toward the Texas School Book Depository. These people have come out specifically to see the President of the United States and here he is in front of them, and they are not looking at him. Why? Because when they heard this sudden loud noise—what sounded like gunfire to some, like a firecracker to others—they instinctively turned toward that sound, toward the Texas School Book Depository. Still others have not yet realized what is happening.

For people who still debate a shooter on the "grassy knoll," I point to this photo. Clearly, the shots came from behind.

The assassination of President Kennedy was the end of a chapter in American history. For a moment, politics and prejudices were forgotten as humanity bonded in unspeakable grief. Although evil had pierced a hole in America's armor, our Constitution provided the framework for the peaceful transition of power, and when President Johnson took the oath of office on Air Force One, it was our democracy at its best.

Then, through the magic of television, the entire world watched the black-veiled thirty-four-year-old widow walk valiantly, her head held high, through the streets of America's capital city, and somehow Jacqueline Kennedy's strength and dignity gave all of us the courage to go on. If she could do it, so could we.

The images are indelible in our collective memory: the courageous widow leading an army of world leaders; the blue-eyed daughter kissing her father's flag-draped casket; and the perfect salute by the three-year-old son of the slain president.

President John F. Kennedy understood that the power of America lies not in its politics—whether you are red or blue—but in its resilience and unified vision of freedom and liberty. One thing I know for sure is that he would not have wanted his legacy, fifty years later, to be a debate about the details of his death. Rather, he would want people to focus on the values and ideals in which he so passionately believed, so that for all Americans, our best days lie ahead.

A man may die, nations may rise and fall, but an idea lives on.

—President John F. Kennedy

Acknowledgments

In October 2012, we were talking to Mitchell Ivers, our brilliant editor at Gallery Books, about the paperback release of *Mrs. Kennedy and Me*, and the conversation turned to what our next project might be. Mitchell had a vision of a book filled with photographs focusing on the days surrounding the assassination, with Clint's memories alongside the dramatic pictures. We knew it would be a difficult book emotionally, but the tremendous response and outpouring of affection we had received from readers of *Mrs. Kennedy and Me* helped us realize that *Five Days in November* was another story that needed to be told, and we began working on it immediately.

Once again, Mitchell, you have guided us through the process with ease and encouragement, always spot-on with your suggestions and comments. You have become a trusted friend, and we are deeply grateful for all you do on our behalf.

The entire team at Gallery Books is responsible for the beauty and design of this book. To President Louise Burke, Publisher Jen Bergstrom, and Jen Robinson, Director of Publicity, thank you for your friendship and support—we are so happy to have you in our corner. Production editor Alexandre Su, Art Director Lisa Litwack, Designer Paul Dippolito, Managing Editor Kevin McCahill, Production Manager Larry Pekarek, and Tom Pitoniak, you did an amazing job of putting our words and pictures into a beautiful and tasteful design that embodies the essence of those historic and tragic days. To Natasha Simons, thank you for pulling all of these parts together, for promptly replying to our endless questions and last-minute additions with professionalism and courtesy. And, last but certainly not least, to Mary McCue, our dedicated publicist, thank you for all you do behind the scenes to get our books in the public eye, for coordinating book signings, media interviews, and travel schedules all over the world, and through all the chaos, for managing to always have a smile on your face.

Finding and sourcing photographs for this book was an enormous task and we couldn't have done it without the help of the following people: Gary Mack, Nicola Longford, Mark Davies, Megan Bryant, and Krishna Shenoy at the Sixth Floor Museum at Dealey Plaza; Matthew Lutts at Associated Press; Jerome Sims at the *Dallas Morning News*; Liza Maddrey; Cathy Spitzenberger at the University of Texas at Arlington; Tom Shelton at the University of Texas, San Antonio; Rob Bardua at the National Museum of the U.S. Air Force. Once again the dedicated staff at the John F. Kennedy Presidential Library and Museum were a great resource. Thanks to Ross Matthei and special thanks to Laurie Austin, who fulfills our last minute requests again and again, and still gives us a hug every time we see her. To Robert Knudsen, Jr., we are so grateful to you for providing the photos taken by your father.

To our intern, Lisa Olson, and our assistant, Abby Biernat—thank you so much for helping us with the foreign landscape of social media and all things Internet. We could not have navigated through them without you.

Thank you to Wyman Harris for your discerning eye, both as a proofreader and in helping us choose the final photos. We so appreciate your knowledge and sincere interest in our projects.

There were times when memories needed to be corroborated and for that we leaned on former Secret Service agents Paul Landis and Tom Wells. We are grateful for your willingness to share your fifty-year-old notes, and more importantly, for your friendship and support.

Finally, to all the readers of *Mrs. Kennedy and Me* who have sent handwritten letters, emails, and Facebook messages, and to those of you we have met around the world at book signings and presentations, it is largely because of your overwhelming support that we had the courage to write this book. While we cannot possibly reply to all the messages, please know that we read, save, and appreciate each and every one.

Lisa McCubbin

To my sons, Connor and Cooper, you make me proud each and every day. Thank you for making my life so rich. I love you more than you can imagine.

To Clint—Even though I did not live through these events, you gave me a rare window into history, painful though it was, and I thank you for your candor through this process. Your memory astounds me. I am honored and privileged—and surely envied by many—to share so much time with you, and despite your disbelief, I cherish every minute. For some reason, we were brought together at the right time in both our lives, and I am so grateful we were. You are extraordinary.

Clint Hill

To the men and women of the U.S. Secret Service, active and retired, your encouragement, support, and interest gave me a special reason to write this book. To those of you who lived through this interval, you have periodically relived these five days time and again as I have. Your pain, anguish, and frustration were equal to mine. We all shared that sense of failure. But we continued on. To those of you who came later, I hope you will understand our dedication to duty, to the office of the President, to the Secret Service, and to this country. Your continued adherence to the words "Worthy of Trust and Confidence" give me pride and hope for the future.

To my sons, Chris and Corey, who suffered through this time period, not fully understanding why your father was never there: We can never regain the time lost, but thank you for your willingness to reconnect. A very special thanks for your support and assistance in personal family matters, making it possible for me to concentrate on this book.

To Lisa McCubbin—you made the reliving of this five-day period much easier than I anticipated. It was an excruciating emotional trip down memory lane, but the end result made it all worthwhile. You are a skilled writer, a dedicated and determined co-author, and a trusted friend and confidant. I would not have written this book, or any book, had it not been for you. Thank you for your patience and your willingness to listen. Your thought-provoking questions brought out information I had been suppressing for decades. I told you the story, but you put the words on the page. You are truly remarkable in every sense of the word. I will never be able to adequately thank you.

Photo Credits